Changing Hearts Changing Communities

Karl Brettig

Published by BeamWords Media, 2023.

While every precaution has been taken in the preparation of this book, the publisher assumes no responsibility for errors or omissions, or for damages resulting from the use of the information contained herein.

CHANGING HEARTS CHANGING COMMUNITIES

First edition. July 15, 2023.

Copyright © 2023 Karl Brettig.

ISBN: 979-8223884439

Written by Karl Brettig.

For this reason I kneel before the Father, from whom every family in heaven and on earth derives its name. I pray that out of his glorious riches he may strengthen you with power through his **Spirit** in your inner being, so that Christ may dwell in your **hearts** through faith. And I pray that you, being rooted and established in love, may have power, together with all the saints, to grasp how wide and long and high and deep is the **agape** of Christ, to know this love that surpasses knowledge—that you may be filled to the measure of all the fullness of God. Now to him who is able to do immeasurably more than all we ask or imagine, according to his power that is at work within us to him be glory in the **ekklesia** and in Christ Jesus throughout all generations.

- St Paul's Letter to the Ephesians (3:14-21, *NIV*)

Contents

Chapter One

Reconnecting with your heart, mind, body, and spirit

Do you sense that much of your life lacks meaning and direction? Are you easily overcome by anxiety and despair? Do you find yourself constantly getting caught up in the moment, or are you defined by a higher purpose? Do you want to see change?

If we want to see change we need to begin with ourselves. How often do we like to point the finger at others and shift the blame for all the problems in the world onto them? It has become the dominant currency on social media and in our daily interactions with others. Countless lives are being torn apart by its venom, but in reality, we are powerless to change anyone except ourselves.

So how does change happen? First of all, we need to identify what needs to change and then we need to look at how we can be empowered to make changes in our lives. The process may start with changing our minds but, as well as changing our minds, we need to experience a change of heart attitude and a strengthening of our spirits.

Most of the time we are aware of what is going on in our body and mind but do we think much about our heart and spirit? True they don't seem as accessible as our body and mind but does that matter? We spent a lot of time developing our bodies and our minds, but how much attention do we give to examining our hearts and becoming strong in spirit?

In a world of elevated anxiety and brokenness many are experiencing today, more than ever we need to take care of our heart and spirit as well as our body and mind to develop the resilience needed to live well. Statistics tell us we are living in the most depressed and anxious generation the world has ever seen.

If we want to see disadvantaged communities pivot for the better, we need to take a long view of what is needed. Intergenerational trauma lies at the heart of the challenges of addressing child abuse, drug and alcohol misuse, family violence, crime, escalation in out-of-home care, hospitalization, and incarceration. When individuals access support and therapy they also need to find a healing community to encourage them in their journey or they will continue to be retraumatised and the cycle of intergenerational trauma will continue.

When we experience trauma in early childhood, the development of our brain is impacted in a manner that lies at the heart of many of the behaviors we struggle with throughout our lives. The **effects of trauma** on our brain development are complex. Connections are made in parts of our brain that should have been wired to function much better, had we been consistently nurtured by the loving care of our parents and caregivers.

None of us experience perfect care in our early childhood and we all, to some extent, have developed disconnects that impact what we end up doing. Our immediate acquaintances usually come to recognize these as dysfunctional behaviors when our relationships develop in adulthood. Seemingly innocuous everyday events can trigger overly intense reactions in our minds and in our bodies. These behaviors often lead to conflict as we repeatedly behave in a manner that causes emotional and sometimes physical pain in those around us.

Adverse childhood experiences

Actions of fathers, including childhood abuse and neglect, impact their children to the third and fourth generations according to the ancient Book of Exodus. (Exodus 20:5) In recent times researchers have come to the same conclusion regarding the inter-generational impact of early childhood trauma. Mothers become much less able to nurture and care for their toddlers and infants when they are living in constant fear and stress, and this may impact on their children for generations.

The insecurity that develops in the child later magnifies the struggle that we all have to change harmful attitudes deeply embedded in our hearts and minds. The impact of domestic violence and abuse in the home during the first one thousand days of a child's life is devastating. Damaging stress hormones are released into the body that severely impacts the wiring in the developing brain and subsequently attitudes of the heart. It takes a lot of very hard work to change these effects, and we need all the help we can get in the process.

Most often the behaviors that result from adverse experiences in early childhood are far from what we would prefer to be doing and we are often mystified as to why we are reacting in the manner that we are, and why it is impacting so severely on others. Our bodies end up doing what our minds don't want them to do. Our minds engage in unhealthy thought patterns that also affect our bodies and are destructive to our relationships. St Paul describes this well in the book of Romans, chapter seven, when he says, "For what I want to do I do not do but what I hate I do". We all struggle with this dilemma to some extent, but the struggle is much greater if we have experienced severe early childhood trauma.

While it is important that we do not use childhood trauma as an excuse for our present behavior it is also important that we come to understand the links between our unhelpful present reactions and adverse childhood experiences. This will help us to better understand what is triggering behaviors that are harmful to others and to begin to work on some strategies to change them. This is usually best done with a competent therapist who understands how to identify and work with complex trauma symptoms.

We also need to work at transforming cycles of intergenerational trauma into intergenerational cycles of nurturing and recovery. All of us can learn to better understand and improve our behaviors through our interactions with others, support groups, prayer, learning conversations, and using the many resources that are available online and in print.

SO HOW DO WE IDENTIFY what is going on in our heart, mind, body, and spirit? It's not that we are made up of separate components, it's rather that the heart, mind, body, and spirit are particular aspects of our existence, life, and consciousness. Our hearts and spirit are the aspects that prove most elusive to researchers in relation to the mind and the body. The heart is more difficult to identify in comparison to the mind, as the mind can more easily be related to the functioning of neural circuits in the brain.

If we define the heart as the motivational centre of our being we discover there is a wide body of psychological research on motivation, although there is considerable variation in the definition of what it is exactly. Interestingly, the heart is the most prevalent of the four entities to be found in the Scriptures where it is mentioned something like 850 times. That is nearly ten times more often than the mind, five times more often than the body, and about four times as often as the spirit. Suffice it to say the heart has been central to much of the thinking about what lies at the motivational core of human behavior for many centuries.

With regard to the spirit, we need to remember that in Hebrew the same word *ruach* is used for the human spirit as is used for the Spirit of God and the same applies to the Greek word *pneuma*. As we shall see this is not entirely accidental, as connection between the human spirit and the Spirit of God has a key role to play in changing our hearts and minds.

A change of heart

When we talk about a change of heart we are usually talking about a change of attitude and that is critical to any conversation about behavioral change. Our circumstances may not change but when our attitude is changed we come to view our circumstances very differently and we are also changed in the process. Attitude change does not come as easily as we would like and there are a number of factors that may contribute.

One of the keys that can help us is gaining an understanding of what lies beneath our present attitudes and the behaviors they tend to precipitate. It is here that we need to examine how the formative events of our early childhood impact our present behavior... and there is much to discover. The brain is like a sponge in the first one thousand days of life from the time of conception. It keenly absorbs every bit of information it receives from what is happening around it and stores that information in the form of neural circuits.

Without going into too much neurological detail, there are parts of the brain that regulate reactions we have to everyday events around us. For example, if we have experienced a healthy, nurturing early childhood our brains are more likely to be wired such that stressful events are processed in a more considered way by the prefrontal cortex. If that has not been the case, circuits that have been wired into our brains through distressing events in early childhood may well interrupt that process.

A pathway direct to our limbic system may have been formed which immediately produces something of a fight or flight response to distressing events. This is because the brain has been wired during past trauma events to do this, rather than being wired to have us gain more perspective on events by first processing it through the prefrontal cortex (Guy-Evans, 2021). That is why it is much easier for secure persons to remain calm in the face of stressful events than those experiencing insecurity.

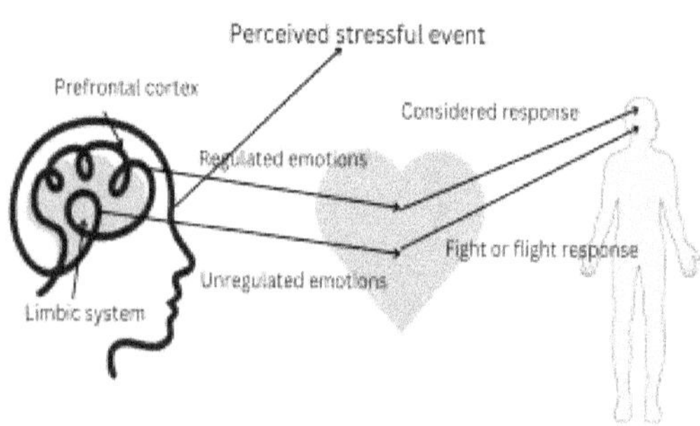

Impact of trauma on brain pathways and behavior

CAN WE CHANGE NEURAL pathways that are triggered by stressful events? The good news is that it is possible and the bad news is that it usually takes a lot of, often painful, therapeutic work. A developing baby is completely unable to process trauma-inducing events in a healthy manner. The impact on the developing brain is very difficult to change, although it is possible.

We need to first come to an understanding of the impact of trauma in early childhood on our present behaviors and then work at rewiring our brain to process past stressful events in a more considered manner, and from an adult perspective. This involves having the courage to identify traumatic early childhood memories and work at integrating these childhood experiences in terms of understanding how they have impacted our mind, heart, and body and then re-framing them from the perspective of an adult.

Symptoms of adverse childhood experiences experienced in the body may include such things as increased heart rates and poor sleep, while the mind may experience intrusive thoughts and bad dreams. These experiences may result in, for example, triggering more intense emotions than the present situations warrant, high levels of anxiety, over-control tendencies, poor impulse control, addictive behaviors, and avoidance of social contact. The goal of therapy is that these symptoms reduce as our mind, body, and heart become more integrated and we experience a more healthy overall sense of self and identity. This generally takes years, even generations, to achieve, depending on the severity of the trauma experienced in our childhood.

The dimension of the spirit

Another avenue that can also play a significant role in overcoming childhood trauma symptoms is the dimension of the spirit (Langberg, 2015, Beauregard & O'Leary, 2008, Yaden & Newberg, 2023). Despite much cybernoise attempting to suggest the contrary, on the basis of relatively few notable failures, research consistently demonstrates a positive correlation between mental health outcomes and religious practices[1] (Fagan, 2006).

Outcomes of religious practices also include improved health attitudes and behaviors[2] (Rew & Wong, 2006), improved psychological adjustment to stress[3] (Ano & Vasconcelles, 2005), improved resilience/coping with parental divorce[4] (Shortz & Worthington, 1994), lower levels of depression symptoms[5] (Wright, Frost, & Wisecarver, 1993), improved suicide prevention[6] (Garroutte, Eva Marie et al. 2003), reduced risky behaviors[7] (Sinha, Witmer, Cnaan & Gelles, 2007), improved educational achievement[8] (Massengill & MacGregor, 2012) and better physical health[9] (Oman & Thoresen, 2005). When you take God out of the picture the

---

1.   https://marripedia.org/effects_of_religious_practice_on_health

2.   https://www.researchgate.net/publication/
7230276_A_Systematic_Review_of_Associations_Among_ReligiositySpirituality_a
nd_Adolescent_Heath_Attitudes_and_Behaviors

3.   https://www.researchgate.net/publication/
8214467_Religious_coping_and_psychological_adjustment_to_stress_A_meta-anal
ysis

4.   https://psycnet.apa.org/record/1994-44919-001

5.   https://psycnet.apa.org/record/1994-13629-001

6.   https://pubmed.ncbi.nlm.nih.gov/12614706/

7.   https://www.researchgate.net/publication/
7102757_Adolescent_Risk_Behaviors_and_Religion_Findings_from_a_National_S
tudy

world becomes a daunting place and it's difficult to have confidence in anything.

Despite some hostile skepticism in some circles in recent times, the God hypothesis remains highly tenable[10]. Science alone is unable to explain either the mystery of consciousness or what lies behind the origin of the universe. The now broadly accepted Big Bang theory has added weight to the Biblical view that the universe had a beginning and recent DNA research suggests that human DNA is too complex to have evolved and must have been preprogrammed (Meyer, 2019). Attempts to dethrone the Creator have historically failed and the dogmatists of the theory of natural selection are now coming under increasing scrutiny. [11]

In ***The Road Less Travelled and Beyond***, M. Scott Peck makes the following observation about much of our daily lives.

An enormous amount of time is spent simply reacting. It's as if we are robots programmed to respond on cue to whatever demands the least time and attention and disregard anything that requires putting in extra time and energy to think.

We skim over the surface thoughtlessly. But we must acknowledge that thinking well is a time-consuming process. We can't expect instant results.

---

8.   https://www.researchgate.net/publication/235271393_Religious_Nonaffiliation_and_Schooling_The_Educational_Trajectories_of_Three_Types_of_Religious_Nones

9.   https://psycnet.apa.org/record/2006-00771-024

10.   https://www.harpercollins.com/products/return-of-the-god-hypothesis-stephen-c-meyer?variant=40352363348002

11.   https://www.theguardian.com/science/2022/jun/28/do-we-need-a-new-theory-of-evolution

We have to slow down a bit and take time to contemplate, meditate even pray. It's the only route to a more meaningful and efficient existence.

In Romans chapter eight, St Paul talked about how the "Law of the Spirit of life set me free from the law of sin and death". Paul, who once heartlessly persecuted Christians, says he was now freed from the domination of his old self and could choose to put on the new self and "not live according to the sinful nature but according to the Spirit".

Acts chapter nine records that this new freedom came after his conversion and infilling with the Holy Spirit on a trip to Damascus while he was "breathing murderous threats against the Lord's disciples". His transformation was remarkable, to say the least. When the Spirit of God indwells our spirit, he says "The Spirit helps us in our weakness. We do not know what we ought to pray for but the Spirit himself intercedes for us with groans that words can not express."

Through prayer, we can become connected to the Giver of Life and be "in the Spirit" rather than "in the flesh". In other words, we no longer need to be dominated by the appetites of the body but can live in the power of the Spirit. A new life that begins with revelation can be maintained by practicing spiritual disciplines, including prayer and worship, as we learn to speak to ourselves and one another in "psalms and hymns and spiritual songs" (See Ephesians 5:18 -20).

This doesn't mean we no longer struggle with symptoms of trauma. The old self has a habit of resurfacing regularly, but we no longer need to be a slave to it (Ludwig & Jacob, 2014). We can daily choose to "set our minds on what the Spirit desires". This can be of great help in overcoming the debilitating effects of past trauma and also in experiencing a life well lived in service of a God who knows our innermost being and has good plans and purposes for our lives.

Inner healing

A practice that is potentially helpful in addressing painful early childhood memories is what is commonly called prayer for inner healing (Davediuk-Gingrich, 2020). It usually involves revisiting childhood memories and bringing them into the presence of Jesus, who bore our griefs and sorrows on the cross, and praying for healing from the emotional pain and suffering inflicted through these events.

This can aid significantly in the healing process, although some caution is needed. For example, praying about one or more memories can not be expected to cover others that may continue to impact the person receiving such prayer. Training and discernment are needed on the part of practitioners involved in this kind of ministry, or a person may become overwhelmed by the experience.

It is best if those involved in such prayer when it relates to painful memories have some understanding of the complexities involved in working with trauma in relation to painful memories. Work also needs to be done to ensure that the person receiving prayer feels safe in the process and with the people involved.

The same cautions also apply to dealing with demonization. Prolonged attempts at deliverance by insufficiently trained people can be very harmful as there are most likely quite a number of other complex issues involved that can not be dealt with in this way. Misdiagnosis can cause a great deal of damage, but that is not to say that many have not profoundly benefited from such a ministry. It is important that those involved in prayer teams work with trained counselors and avail themselves of competent mentoring, training, and supervision.

There is a very well-known verse in Psalm 51 that sums up our need for God to work in our heart, mind, and spirit as we commune in prayer. David prays "Create in me a pure heart O God and renew a steadfast spirit within me". All of our attempts at living within our own capacity usually end up in failure and despair, yet we stubbornly continue to try to live in our own strength, trying to pull ourselves up by our own bootstraps.

Our hearts are prone to deception. According to the prophet Jeremiah, "The heart is deceitful above all things and beyond cure" (Jeremiah 17:9). Despite our best intentions we end up doing what we hate to do. We may be always learning but never able to come to a full knowledge of the truth that sets us free. The deceptive nature of our hearts is also such that we have a strong tendency to use the trauma of our childhood as an excuse for poor present behavior. That is a sure pathway to more misery and pain. Our past may determine our trial in life but it does not have to determine our fate.

Attempts to change our way of thinking as a purely mental process usually fail in the long term. It's so easy to revert back to old patterns of thinking. The more pronounced the disconnect between the heart and the mind the greater the **disconnect between what we say and what we do**. It's amazing how a change of attitude in the motivational centre of our being, which is the heart, can bring about a change of mind and a new way of thinking. As we take responsibility for our actions, rather than trying to shift the blame onto others, our minds are freed to think about and see others in a new light, and we become more responsive to them.

Spiritual disciplines

Learned spiritual disciplines are key to maintaining a softened heart and a thankful attitude in place of what may have become a prison of bitterness and resentment. We can become free from the appetites of the body and the tyrannies of the mind. Regularly reconnecting with God in prayer is a spiritual discipline we need to learn. This practice empowers us to live a life empowered by the Spirit of God engaging with our spirit, changing our hearts, renewing our minds, and producing fruitful actions that positively impact the lives of others.

PROFOUND CHANGE OFTEN comes when we face up to our self-centred way of living, admit our failures, ask God for forgiveness and let go of control in the place of prayer, no matter how little or unsure our faith. We may well then experience a revelation in our minds or an intervention into our circumstances seen through the eyes of faith. The process of change that begins with a prayer of surrender that establishes a connection with God, and a budding faith begins to grow as it is nurtured through spiritual disciplines (Foster, 1978).

The power to change does not come from within ourselves but from the cross of Christ that secured atonement for our wrongdoing and by the Spirit empowers us to live a renewed life. In the Book of Acts in the original Greek language, God is described as the Heart Knower (Gk *cardiognosta*). We find the early believers using that term when they prayed (Acts 1:24). St Peter also used it when he spoke of the Gentiles being given the Holy Spirit when he purified their hearts by faith (Acts 15:8-9).

When we open up the Scriptures faith comes into context, bringing revelation and understanding of God's plan and purpose for our lives. As we meditate on God's Word and what it means for our lives, our hearts and minds become more aligned with that purpose and we experience the reality of God's Spirit interacting with our spirit. A new way of living, that begins with revelation, flourishes as we learn to practice spiritual disciplines and become transformed by the renewal of our minds and changed attitudes in our hearts.

The process of change needs to continue throughout our lives as we pray, meditate, and engage in therapeutic relational and community support. If we are not moving forward spiritually and relationally, we usually end up going backward. Stagnation is not a good option. In the process, we need to be careful about allowing ourselves to look to spiritual experiences to maintain our progress, rather we need to develop a growing trust and faith in the presence of the Heart Knower who is able to do far more than we can ever ask for or even imagine.

We live in a world that delivers excellent medical resources that aid in healing our bodies, and to a lesser extent our minds, but it is our hearts and spirits that also need attention. As well as medical diagnoses of what is happening in our bodies, and identifying the impact of thought patterns in our minds, we need to regularly examine what influences are affecting **our spirit's ability to bring our hearts and minds into alignment**. As we daily identify these influences and admit to our failures in the place of prayer and meditation on the living God and Word, we are likely to experience a change in our heart attitude and find ourselves living more productive and fulfilling lives.

What we have looked at in these pages clearly does not cover the full complexity of our human existence, though it does offer some important keys to understanding ourselves and others. We have not even considered the term *psyche* which is the Greek word from which psychology is derived. Generally speaking, we can say it includes aspects of the mind and heart and is usually thought of in terms of the mind, will, and emotions.

Though the function of the *psyche* incorporates much of what we have considered, what we have here is an attempt to understand key aspects of our day-to-day existence in a not-too-complicated manner, to help us negotiate the challenges of our daily lives. The Book of Hebrews (Hebrews 4:12) suggests we need to delve deeply into the living Word of God to learn the difference between the *psyche* (soul) and the *pneuma* (spirit). There we have an ever-revealing mirror that helps us to see what is in our hearts and minds and is impeding our spiritual life.

There is much to learn about each of the concepts we have introduced, and we will further explore them in the following chapters. What is important though is that we try to put into practice what have learned, while at the same time remaining in the process of continuing to learn.

Chapter Two
Examining the Heart

There is a primary reason we have so much conflict in families, communities, and among nations. We all have desires that battle within us. We all want things for ourselves and we fight and quarrel when we don't get them.

Much of social media activity echoes inflammatory accusations leveled against anyone who differs from our perception of what we see as important. Our nature is such that we prefer to cast aspersions on whoever else we can for the injustices that stare us all in the face, rather than take any personal responsibility for our own contributions to the evolving mess.

If anyone dares suggest that what we are doing may be wrong we fight back with vitriol and slander and cancel out any further engagement with them. We hide behind **manufactured speech codes** to insulate ourselves from a meaningful conversation as we impose our views on others and troll anyone who dares to dissent from them with targeted precision.

Many online communities are in a perpetual state of war because of a lack of consensus. Social media has become a battleground for culture wars between individuals and groups who seek to promote their personal agendas and self-interests in contested areas such as class, race, and sexual preference. Tolerance is weaponized to justify intolerance against particular nonconforming groups. Why do we find it so difficult to accept responsibility for the obvious failings we all have? Why do we always have to be right?

The problem begins in early childhood. We come into the world as totally dependent infants. Our every need needs to be taken care of and our default strategy of making sure we are fed and have our nappies changed regularly is to cry when we are feeling uncomfortable, a perfectly functional behavior. However, a time soon comes when we need to be weaned and toilet trained. That is when parents and carers need to take a more assertive training role in all aspects of the life of the developing child. If we are not trained in our early years, we continue to operate as demanding infants into adulthood.

Quality of life depends on heart attitudes

Demanding infants try to dominate and control parents and caregivers. If we succeed we continue on in life as a demanding child. We try to dominate and control our playmates. If we succeed we continue to use this strategy to bully others in our adult lives, whether we are conscious of doing this or not.

All of this time we are carefully observing the reactions of our parents and caregivers and later our teachers. If they themselves have been abused or neglected in their early years most will have issues that limit the quality of their caregiving. Rather than building character and healthy attitudes in children, they may well end up trying to use them to meet unmet needs brought about by their own early childhood deprivation.

Parents and caregivers have a very major role to play in the character and attitude formation of the children entrusted to them. Whatever they lack in terms of providing **nurture and boundaries** will severely impact the lives of their children. So we all need to look below the surface at what is underlying the attitudes we have developed toward others in our adult lives.

The quality of our lives depends very much upon us regularly examining what is underlying our heart attitudes (Willard, 2021). Childhood insecurity breeds adult domination and control but, on the other hand, childhood security can also contribute to a limited ability to express authentic emotions and be sensitive to the needs of others. None of us are exempt from the need for a regular examination of our hearts.

Examining the issues of life

Don't we hate examinations? They bring back memories of those times in our lives when the amount of work we have done at school or in further education is put under the microscope in order to see how well we have learned. They are times of reckoning designed to measure what we have actually learned in our studies and are developed to override our innate ability to evade the truth.

So what is an examination of the heart? If you Google the subject you will find a lot of information from cardiologists about the need to keep tabs on the health of your heart because your very life depends upon it. But interestingly, of some 850 mentions of the heart in the Hebrew books of the Old Testament only a few of them refer to the physical organ.

The Book of Proverbs (4:23) instructs us to take guard of our hearts because it is the wellspring of life. The Hebrew word for wellspring used here is *totsaoth* and it is derived from the word we would usually translate as 'issues' or more literally 'outgoings' of life. What comes out of the heart has a huge influence on our daily lives.

The heart is at the centre of our being where impulses that impact the direction of our lives are formed. We all have issues and they all have consequences so we all need to take guard of our hearts. Those who play the game of cricket take guard every time they go out to face the opposing bowlers. They need to know where their stumps targeted by the bowlers are in relation to their bodies in order to reduce the chances of being dismissed. We also need to take guard of our hearts if we do not wish to be easily dismissed by our adversaries.

Our hearts are as important as our heads in an age when a cerebral focus tends to dominate our academic conversations. As conservative Winston Churchill once quipped with regard to liberal ideology, "You have no head if you wholly embrace it, but if you categorically reject it, you have no heart". We need to take both perspectives into our consideration.

Perceptual blindness

If cardiologists encourage us to have regular checkups more so do we need to take a look at what underlies the issues we face in our lives. The problem for most of us is that we are perceptually blind. Some would say perpetually blind but that doesn't have to be the case. Others are much better at seeing our blind spots than we are and we can learn a lot from their observations if we are serious about recognizing the depth of our childish, self-centred attributes.

Psychiatrists look to the *Diagnostic and Statistical Manual of Mental Disorders (DSM)* to identify dysfunctional behaviors in our lives. The *DSM* may diagnose ailments but it does not address the meaning and purpose of life nor does it assign particular responsibility for our behaviors.

Many psychologists tend to believe that it is our feelings that determine meaning in relation to our actions. The focus in therapy accordingly is often on gaining emotional intelligence by getting in touch with underlying feelings. While that may be helpful it is only a partial exploration of the whole process needed to find healing.

More recently some argue that **perceptual intelligence** is the latest frontier in the search for living a more fulfilled life. We flourish in our relationships when we emerge from perceptual blindness and begin to see where we may be, or are, wrong. We can then work at changing the things about us that cause us to lose our grip on life.

Though most of us did not enjoy school examinations and prefer to avoid them as adults, they are an important means of evaluating our progress. An examination at school assesses what we have learned through what we have studied. An examination of the heart seeks to identify blind spots that may be negatively impacting our relationships and quality of life.

The unexamined life

Socrates' well-known dictum "The unexamined life is not worth living" continues to echo its worth through the ages. Most of us stumble through life in a fog of our own making. If are drifting aimlessly through the mist and spend our lives crashing into one brick wall after another, we eventually do not have much left about our life that is worth living. Sadly that is the road many travel, neglecting to take stock of what is driving their behavior before the pain of an unexamined life eventually becomes overwhelming.

A common evasion of responsibility is to hide behind a moral relativism that points to the failures of others in order to justify our own. Such a strategy enables us to deflect from owning up to what we know to be wrong by suggesting others are doing it so it can't be all that bad. So we carry on as if there are no consequences to bear and continue on our merry way as the consequences of our behavior gradually overtake us.

We become addicted to **anger and resentment** as it rises within our hearts when we are unable to control dissenters who come across our path. Our minds and eventually our bodies become infected by this insidious poison. Our hearts become dark places as our minds are preoccupied with strategizing vengeance on those who disagree with our greedy ambitions, hopes, and plans.

The consequences of bitterness are regularly reported in accounts of the tragic lives of many who we once thought had everything to live for, but whose lives ended prematurely and in miserable circumstances. Overindulgence in gratifying the lust of the eyes and the pride of life weaves an all-consuming web of self-destruction. It usually goes unreported in the lives of the many who reach the end wondering what their life has been all about.

The examined life

We need to be able to identify the behaviors in our lives that are causing harm to us and others and are out of line with the way we were meant to live. We need to turn away from evil and be able to change our hearts and minds about doing what we know to be wrong.

The Master taught us that the examined life begins with a heart inspection. According to the account in Mark (7:21-22) out of the heart come evil thoughts, pornography, theft, murder, adultery, greed, hatred, deceit, lewdness, envy, slander, arrogance, and folly. Amazing how this first-century list includes much of what we see on today's social media platforms, television, film, and print media.

These are the things, that according to verse 23, that 'defile' us and make us dysfunctional. The concept of us being defiled triggers political and moral outrage in many contemporary hearts and minds, as indeed has always been the case. We usually prefer a version of optimistic humanism and do anything to avoid facing up to blind spots in our hearts. It makes us very uncomfortable.

To see the concept of sin as a social construction rather than a moral failure is very appealing. We would much rather attempt to devise our own **moral framework** from human resources than recognize a divine source. Anything that challenges the popular view of political correctness is greeted with outrage and contempt by those who prowl social media for dissenters from their opinions.

Interestingly, the list begins with evil thoughts which we would normally associate with the activity of neurons in the brain. Scientific studies however have discovered that there are approximately 40,000 brain-like neurons in the actual heart. They communicate with the brain as do neurons found in other organs.

Evil thoughts may lead us into the vices listed here, or many others as well unless something is done to interrupt the process. Mature adults may have a well-developed prefrontal cortex in the brain that is readily able to dismiss very dark thoughts without too much trouble, but it is amazing how many of us fall into many of the less obvious sins.

Ignatian Spirituality brought us *The Examen* which teaches twice daily prayerful reflection on our thoughts and daily events to bring them into focus in the light of the presence of God. Other heart examination practices include regularly taking personal responsibility for our actions rather than blame-shifting, delaying gratification, practicing gratitude, practicing forgiveness, and dedication to the truth.

Wrongdoing

Our tendency in an age of moral relativism is to rationalize some forms of wrongdoing as a lifestyle choice we are free to make. While that may temporarily alleviate some of the guilt we may experience, in the long term it does not prevent the harmful consequences of the choices we make. The real tragedy is that sin harms the loving relationship we were meant to have with our Creator and Sustainer, irrespective of the social and emotional damage we may be doing to ourselves when we make choices that don't align with how we were created to live.

So what are the things that come out of our hearts that mess with our minds, defile us, make us dysfunctional, and separate us from God? Let's look at a few of them. The first on the list is probably the most flaunted one littered across the internet and likely one of the most challenging we encounter every day. The Greek word used to describe it in the book of

Mark is *porneia.* from which we get the word pornography. It also can be translated as sexual immorality.

Here we are moving into an area that opens up a hornet's nest of contemporary controversy, particularly since the sixties attempted repudiation of the doctrine of original sin in favor of living a permissive lifestyle. Several books of the Bible call *porneia* sin. There's that 's 'word again. It causes a lot of self-righteous indignation to rise up in those who hear it especially when it may relate to their behavior. How dare we call it out as such.

While in the short term, it may be more comfortable to avoid the concept of right and wrong, in the long term the consequences of avoiding the truth are very harmful to individuals and communities. Sin is like cancer that eats away at our relationship with God as we try to justify our poor behaviors and cancel out anyone who questions it in an effort to alleviate the guilt we experience because of it. The corrosive energy we expend in trying to do that significantly impacts our wellbeing.

The truth is we are all guilty of sin. The Master made that pretty clear in the Sermon on the Mount. "You have heard that it was said, 'Do not commit adultery. But I tell you that anyone who looks at a woman lustfully has already committed adultery with her in his heart" (Matthew 5:27-28). How many of us haven't done that?

We are all sinners. St Paul stated this in his letter to the Romans when he said "For all have sinned and fallen short of the glory of God (3:23). Sin simply means wrongdoing. What begins in the heart is entertained in the mind and acted out in the body, and we are all caught up in it to some degree or another.

Theft

Again haven't we all done it? Most of what is written here isn't entirely original Many minds far greater than mine have pondered the depths of the issues of life we are considering and written up their observations. For the sake of brevity, I've opted to reference some of my most relevant sources at the end as further reading though I know there are many others that could have been included.

With AI-created content now approved for use in tertiary examinations where will our propensity for plagiarism end? We are all fast becoming very sophisticated thieves and robbers. Of course, we can readily point the finger at those guilty of far worse indiscretions but that doesn't excuse us from plenty of our own.

Murder

If we go to the Master's observations on murder in the Sermon on the Mount again we find ourselves in trouble. Anger is placed in the same category as murder and how many of us have never become angry?

"You have heard that it was said to the people long ago, 'You shall not murder, and anyone who murders will be subject to judgement.' But I tell you that anyone who is angry with a brother or sister will be subject to judgement" (Mathew 5:21-22). Now, this is getting challenging. Did the Master come to just condemn us all? No, he came to free us from ourselves and to connect us to a new way of living in forgiveness and empowered by the Spirit.

Greed

Greed is wanting more than we need. We usually associate it with money but its insidious grip extends far beyond money, houses, and conveniences. It can also be about wanting more attention and respect than we need. We can be set free from such all-consuming greed.

The Master said 'whoever loses his life for my sake will find it" (Mathew 16:35). We need to turn away from the allure of the things we desire but do not need, and by giving them away we will no longer be nourishing the greed that once gripped our hearts and minds. At least until the next temptation comes along.

Folly

The Greek word used for folly literally means a lack of moral and intellectual sense. How much of what we do lacks basic common sense? How often do we get involved in too many senseless activities?

Are our lives meant to be consumed by an endless procession of indulging in fruitless bread and circuses? Do we manage our screen time or does it manage us? Are we managing our priorities sensibly? Much of what we do, in the final analysis, lacks a lot of common sense.

Arrogance

CS Lewis saw that pride and self-conceit open up the door to all other vices and is the utmost evil – the complete anti-God state of mind. "If you think you are not conceited you are very conceited indeed". It is the opposite of humility. The more pride we have in ourselves the more we dislike seeing it in others. Humility frees us from "strutting about like the little idiots we are" (Lewis, 2009).

"I wish I had gone a bit further with humility myself. If I had I could probably tell you more about the relief, the comfort, of taking the fancy dress off - getting rid of the false self, with all its 'Look at me' and 'Aren't I a good boy?' and all its posing and posturing." - *Mere Christianity*

This is the kind of talk that goes against the grain of much popular thought. We'll do anything we can to avoid recognising the dark side of our nature in our hunger for affirmation and 'likes'. The reasons for our heightened sense of self-obsession may well lie in the paucity of the nurture we received in our early childhood.

The insecurity that stems from poor attachment and lack of bonding in the early years is debilitating in relation to our self-confidence. It makes it very difficult for us to face up to the frailties of our nature, even though doing this is one of the most liberating things we can possibly aim to do. That is why Freud pointed out that an inferiority complex is often masked as apparent superiority.

Guilt and shame

Wrongdoing weighs us down with guilt and shame and can easily crush our spirit. We need to learn to distinguish between guilt and shame, self-denial and self-hatred. Guilt says I've done something bad, shame says I am bad. Sustained abuse can cause a lot of damage in terms of how we see ourselves, and a debilitating sense of shame may be the result.

Shame elicits feelings of powerlessness and worthlessness and a sense of being exposed while false guilt comes from things we have not actually done. Both shame and false guilt can lead to feelings of self-hatred and that is debilitating. On the other hand self-denial and delaying gratification is an entirely good discipline to exercise.

Confession, forgiveness, and change

A healthy kind of guilt motivates us to identify wrongdoing and deal with it by admitting to offenses and receiving forgiveness. When we identify our wrongdoing, apologize, and ask for forgiveness the matter can be resolved with an 'I forgive you' from the offended party. That doesn't usually mean that total trust is immediately restored but it is a good place to start the process.

Forgiveness is powerful. We forgive because we have been forgiven of so much because of what Christ endured on the cross of Calvary in order that we might be forgiven. It was our wrongdoing that put him there and needed to be atoned for, and that leaves us with no reason not to forgive others (Keller, 2022).

Forgiveness takes away any excuse from us to retaliate when we are mistreated by others and makes us in fact 'unoffendable'. We have no need to hold on to resentment and bitterness or take part in acts of revenge. That doesn't mean we don't have boundaries in place or that we minimize abuse from others, but what it does mean is that we free ourselves from downward spirals of self-pity and depressive thinking.

Regardless of the responses we receive from those we forgive what is most important is that we come clean, admit our own sins before God, and receive the forgiveness secured by Christ on the cross. That is what sets us free from the burden of guilt and shame that can weigh so heavily on our hearts. It is the central message of the cross that needs to be received by all. Jesus Christ has paid the ultimate price for our wrongdoing and the power to change stems from that pivotal event in history.

Coming clean before God involves a major renovation of the heart. Repentance (a change of mind accompanied by sorrow for wrongdoing) doesn't mean feeling sorry for ourselves. It is what St Paul calls Godly sorrow that leads to repentance and salvation, while worldly sorrow leads to death (2 Corinthians 7:10).

Paul wrote about this in the context of having previously sent a very confronting letter addressing some very serious issues in the Corinthian community. Sometimes we also need to be confronted with some hard truths in order to come to a place of heartfelt repentance and experience the joy that it brings.

The softened heart

The good news is that redemption from wrongdoing has been made possible and our hearts can be cleaned and renewed by the Spirit of God as we become convicted of wrongdoing and moved to repentance. Once hard hearts can be softened by the grace and forgiveness we receive through the atonement of Jesus.

Our lives can be transformed as we learn to forgive others just as we have been forgiven. We see this in the Lord's Prayer (Mathew 6:9-15) and we are now also seeing it further validated in recent Positive Psychology research as well as countless testimonies of transformed lives.

A change of heart comes about as we own up to our wrongdoing and ask God to forgive us in the place of prayer. It is there that we find redemption and the weight of our misdeeds taken from us through the cross of sacrifice.

Our hearts are softened by the amazing **love of God** and as we become sensitized to our wrongdoing. We become more aware of the deception and evil desires within our hearts that give birth to sin (James 1:13-15). When we are touched by the love of God, ingrained strongholds of evil behavior patterns can be overcome.

What is this love of God? A lot is said, written, and sung about love and it comes in many forms. Sexual love (Greek *eros*) is often at the forefront as is familial, brotherly, or sisterly love (*phileo*). The loving presence of God (*agape)* however is what we are talking about here and it has to do with the very nature of God. God in fact is love (1 John 4:16) and loves us so much that he was willing to sacrifice his Son (John 3:16) to save us from eternal death.

We were created to know God's continuous *agape* love for us, and it is that love that can overcome the forces of evil that bring about the destruction and chaos we see all around us. Change begins in our hearts as we are set free from our obsession with our old selves and begin to live in the presence of our Creator and Redeemer.

Our predisposition to sin is overcome by love, and other fruits of the Spirit such as joy, peace, kindness, goodness, gentleness, and mercy. This doesn't mean we become free from our old selves and predisposition to selfish behavior. The old self still lurks beneath the surface ready to resume control of our lives when we lose our focus on the Giver of Life and his plan and purpose for us.

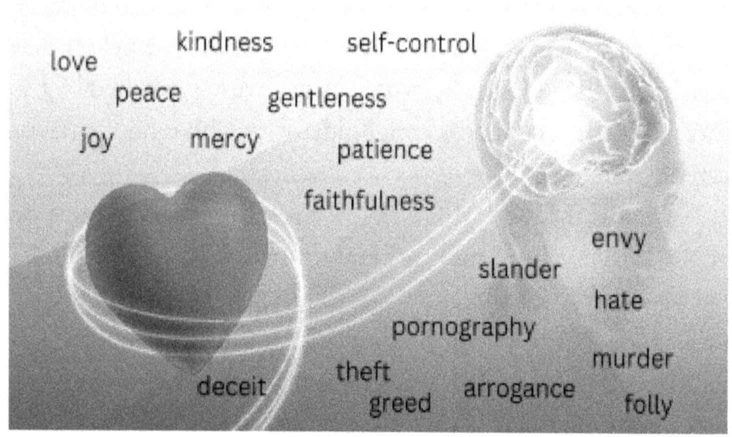

BLESSED ATTITUDES

What attitudes should we long to have cultivated in our hearts? The Master gave us some important clues in the Sermon on the Mount (Mathew 5:3-12). We are blessed when we are poor in spirit. That means we have become aware that we are bankrupt before God in ourselves. We actually become strong when we recognize the poverty in ourselves.

We mourn when we recognize the wrongdoing and its consequences in our lives. We are blessed when we become meek - and that does not mean weak. When we are surrendered to God we experience a strength that God gives us that is not our own. It comes when we humble ourselves, the antithesis of being proud and arrogant.

We are blessed when we hunger and thirst not for food and drink but for living the life that we were created to live. That is a life cultivated by the Spirit of God and we need to hunger for this to happen in our lives. It is not a life that we can live by our own strength so we are blessed when we hunger for God to fill us with the Spirit. We can cultivate such an attitude through prayer and fasting and developing an appetite for the Word of God.

We are blessed when we show mercy and have an attitude of forgiveness toward others. How we treat others comes back to us. Mathew 7:12 instructs us to do to others as we would have them do to us and that sums up the essence of the Old Testament law and prophetic writings.

We are blessed when our hearts are made clean and our eyes are opened to see God at work in and around us. If our desire is to see more of God we need to ask him to purify our hearts. That refinement process may be painful as we come to see the depth of selfishness and deceitfulness in our hearts.

We are blessed when we aim to have a calming influence on others in the storms of life and pursue peace. We are blessed when we are persecuted in our efforts to do this. That is a time to rejoice rather than feel sorry for ourselves if the persecution comes because we choose to follow in the way of the Master.

Cultivation

When we strive for new heart attitudes simply in our own strength we usually end up falling flat on our faces. They are cultivated when we open up ourselves to the Spirit of God to connect with our spirit by letting go and surrendering our will to God's plans for our life.

Such radical humility empowers us to flourish and live in the flow of the Spirit. We find this concept now being developed in Positive Psychology though it tends to fall short with regard to understanding how such flow actually germinates and takes place.

One of the best analogies for the process of transformation is the emergence of a butterfly from a cocoon. It is literally reborn as a new creature that can spread its wings and fly. Another is that of a seed that must be planted in the ground and die before new sprouts appear as it is sprinkled with water, and emerges to grow by taking in air and sunlight.

The Master spoke of this process (John 12:23), endured the pain of crucifixion, and emerged from the grave to announce that the rule of evil and the curse of wrongdoing has been broken. He promised to be with his followers as they were sent out to announce this good news.

We too need to let go of our old life, surrender it to Jesus, and allow him to lead and guide us in our daily lives. Surrender involves a radical humility that acknowledges our weakness before God in order that the power of Christ might impact our lives. Our old self needs to be crucified, releasing a life of faith and obedience to God, and the new self needs to be nurtured by the Spirit through the mentoring of mature disciples, daily meditation on the Scriptures, and a life of prayer.

Jesus promised he would not leave us as orphans in search of our identity (John 14:18). As many today crave to be loved and accepted by peers and look to alternative lifestyles, therapies, and medical interventions in their search for identity, God promises to send the Spirit of truth to comfort, counsel and convict (John 16:7-11). The truth is we were all made to be in a relationship with God and that relationship is sealed by the agency of the Holy Spirit coming into our lives.

One of the dangers of the present time is that we have inherited the social justice fruits of Christianity such as care for the sick, the poor, and the oppressed even if we no longer believe in, or see a need for God. If we continue to remain distant from God, our lives will most likely gradually disintegrate over time, as will our communities.

We need to understand that God loves us to the extent that he was prepared to give up his only Son to die for us in order that we might come to know His good plan and purpose for our lives, both for now and in eternity (John 3:16).

When we water a seed new growth begins to emerge from the soil, breathe in the air, and photosynthesise in the light. So it is when the Spirit brings us to life, breathes into our spirit, and frees us to walk in the light. Our heart attitudes begin to change as darkness in our lives is overcome by the truth and light of the living Word. We become free to live the fulfilling and productive life we were created to live.

Chapter Three
Living by the Spirit

When it comes to the human spirit researchers find it very challenging to define what it actually is or even if it exists. It must exist in some form because when it leaves us we die. On one level the same Greek word *pneuma* is used for breath as is used for spirit and we obviously can't live without the ability to breathe. On another level when we lose consciousness our bodies may still be breathing but our minds no longer function. Science has a lot of difficulty explaining what consciousness exactly is, as it does with explaining the human spirit. Clearly, it is more than just breathing although, interestingly, the same word Hebrew word *ruach* is also used for breath as it is for spirit in the books of the Old Testament.

The Master said that the Spirit of God is like the wind that blows wherever it wants. "You hear its sound but you can not tell where it comes from or where it is going. So it is with everyone born of the Spirit" (John 3:8). In relation to this, he makes a distinction between *pneuma* and *sarkos* or **spirit and flesh.** The flesh is literally the material that covers our bones but it also refers to our human or sinful nature. St Paul goes on to develop this teaching in his letter to the Galatians, surely one of the most revolutionary letters ever written. Let's take a look at what he says (Galatians 5:16-25).

16 So I say, walk by the Spirit, and you will not gratify the desires of the flesh. 17 For the flesh desires what is contrary to the Spirit, and the Spirit what is contrary to the flesh. They are in conflict with each other so that you are not to do whatever you want. 18 But if you are led by the Spirit, you are not under the law.

19 The acts of the flesh are obvious: sexual immorality, impurity, and debauchery; 20 idolatry and witchcraft; hatred, discord, jealousy, fits of rage, selfish ambition, dissensions, factions 21 and envy; drunkenness, orgies, and the like. I warn you, as I did before, that those who live like this will not inherit the kingdom of God.

22 But the fruit of the Spirit is love, joy, peace, forbearance, kindness, goodness, faithfulness, 23 gentleness and self-control. Against such things there is no law. 24 Those who belong to Christ Jesus have crucified the flesh with its passions and desires. 25 Since we live by the Spirit, let us keep in step with the Spirit.

St Paul writes this in the context of having previously elaborated on the pitfalls of trying to keep the law by ourselves rather than relying on the Spirit to empower our daily walk. He argues that having been reborn of water and the Spirit we have been freed from the entrapment of the law and trying to reach perfection by human effort.

In another letter, he expounds on the need to be filled with the Spirit and to speak to one another "In psalms and hymns and spiritual songs, singing and making music in our heart to the Lord" (Ephesians 5:19-21). The ability to do this is a result of a crucified flesh with all its passions and desires and living a life filled with the Spirit. It includes "always giving thanks in everything"...and the Greek word *panton* used here means all things. That is a challenge in a world in which we constantly encounter difficult circumstances.

The challenge of refusing to gratify the flesh pales in comparison to the joy of experiencing the fruit of being filled with the Spirit. The promise is that we will not gratify the flesh, as is our constant temptation if we walk by the Spirit. As spiritual babies, we are not good at that but we can learn. Giving thanks in everything, for example, is a spiritual discipline very foreign to our flesh. Positive Psychology introduces us to virtues such as gratitude, but this somewhat more radical teaching takes it to another level.

A few decades ago there was a decorated US Army officer called Merlin Carothers who ended up in a penitentiary where he discovered the profound truth of praising God regardless of circumstances. It transformed his life and he went on to write a book called *Prison to Praise and* ended up selling over nineteen million copies of his books as well as helping an army of people in the process, including by giving free books to many prisoners.

We too can be free from prisons of resentment and bitterness by practising forgiveness and taking up this important discipline of praising God regardless of circumstances. We don't allow our circumstances to shape our perception of God in a conflicted world. In times of significant pain, we turn to the Comforter who reminds us of the true nature of God rather than allow ourselves to be drowned by a spiral of unbelief. It doesn't change our loss but it heals our perspective.

Positive Psychology has developed the concept of flow that attempts to describe a state of being in which we are functioning at our best. When we walk in the Spirit we can experience a strong sense of being guided and led by the Spirit. We can flow in the Spirit as we focus our attention on Jesus and his promise to be with us always, as we use the spiritual gifts he gives us and exercise the spiritual disciplines he taught.

Our Creator is not reluctant to give us the gifts of the Spirit (1 Corinthians 12:1-11) but we need to ask for them (Luke 11:13). There has been much debate among faith communities over their availability for today, however in recent decades research and practice has, by and large, validated their use which is now widely accepted in the Christian community worldwide. There has been a corresponding upsurge in the exercise of the gifts over the past century. Again a change of heart and mind is needed if we are to make use of the gifts of the Spirit that have been made available to us.

A clash of worldviews

In the Scriptures, the Spirit is referred to as the Holy Spirit nearly a hundred times specifically in the New Testament. The New Testament also acknowledges the presence of other spirits that are decidedly unholy. They are evil spirits or demons and they persistently work against the activity of the Holy Spirit in our lives. This may come as a surprise to those of us who have been educated and trained to hold a naturalistic worldview.

Naturalism presupposes that the supernatural doesn't exist, so any talk of evil spirits is considered to be a primitive delusion. This view has dominated in the West since eighteenth-century rationalism took hold in most academic institutions, including many theological seminaries. It remains foreign to those in many countries that have maintained traditional worldviews regarding supernatural activity and those engaged in New Age activities.

That is not to deny that many significant and liberating developments have come out of eighteenth-century enlightenment views. Religious faith does not exclude scientific knowledge but rather it includes it in terms of an interactive relationship. However, in some circles, there has been much of an over-correction regarding traditional beliefs and practices, that has led to the almost total exclusion of recognising the spiritual dimension of life.

In *The Screwtape Letters,* CS Lewis had this to say about finding a balance. "There are two equal and opposite errors our race can fall into about the devils. One is to disbelieve in their existence. The other is to believe and then feel an excessive and unhealthy interest in them".

In the meantime, paranormal practices have re-emerged in the mainstream as the New Age movement has gained prominence in recent years. Alternative medicine and Eastern mysticism have thrived as **scientism**, a view that sees science as a closed system and the only way to truth, suffocated our innate longing for connection with a world beyond ourselves.

The probability of the non-existence of God is about $1:10^{100}$, as that is the estimated probability of the fine-tuning required for the Big Bang theory to be true. Meanwhile, the tales of Harry Potter have captivated the hearts and minds of children in the same manner the CS Lewis tales of Narnia once did. Today talk of facing our demons abounds, but how well do we understand the supernatural reality behind our struggles?

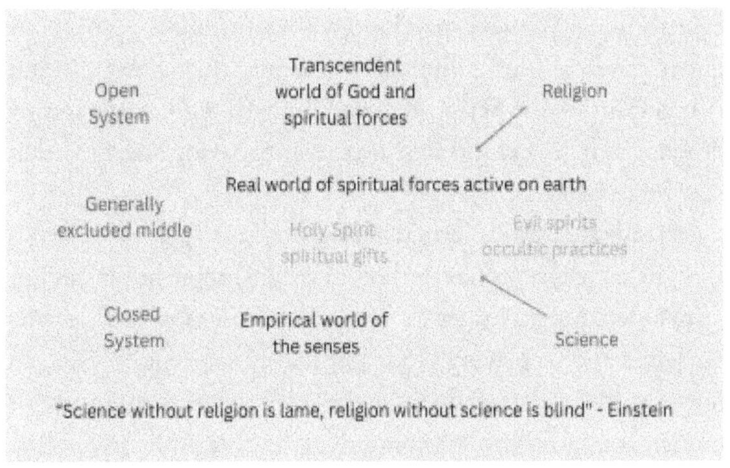

Worldviews that may be influencing our thought processes

IN HIS LETTER TO THE Ephesians St Paul writes that "Our struggle is not against flesh and blood but against principalities and powers, against the rulers of this present darkness, against the spiritual forces of evil in the heavenly realms" (Ephesians 6:12). To those immersed in scientism this is fantasy but to those confronted by their demons and wanting to be free to live a productive life, it rings of truth. It provides another perspective on the enormous penetration of dysfunctional beliefs, ideologies, behaviors, and disasters that ravage the world.

Of course, for those at either end of the spectrum, a predisposition to overemphasis lurks, but, as Einstein suggested, we need to be able to integrate the wisdom of both science and faith into our worldview. What begins with greed, envy, hatred and selfish ambition in the heart gives birth to deathly evil, perpetrated by those who fall into major deception. While psychology contributes to our understanding of human personality, habits, and vulnerabilities, the Scriptures contribute to our understanding of what may lie behind dysfunctional behavior and how that may be addressed.

Hindrances to spiritual growth

The concept of sin is not a comfortable topic but it can not be avoided. Sin separates us from God. It lures us into serving ourselves and to playing God, and that is a deception. We can not possibly understand all the complexities of the universe or human consciousness. As computer scientists aspire to develop Artificial General Intelligence to fill the information gaps and reassure the world that we have everything under control, anxiety continues to soar and insecurity reigns.

The first uncomfortable truth we must face up to if we are to grow spiritually is the presence of sin in our lives. It must be identified and acknowledged before God and in some cases before others that we have offended. That is where we find forgiveness (1 John: 1:9-10) and healing (James 5:16).

The second main hindrance to spiritual growth is the presence in our lives of any spirits other than the Holy Spirit. Any engagement with occult activities and idol worship needs to be acknowledged and renounced if we are to grow spiritually. This is not a popular assertion but one that has been attested in the lives of many who have found the freedom that renouncing such practices brings (Anderson, 1990).

The fact is that everybody holds a set of exclusive beliefs and the real question is which set of beliefs can produce the most peace-loving, reconciling, and inclusive behavior. The message of Christianity calls to make an admission that we are no better than anyone else. That message came through the One who endured a cross, loved and sacrificially served others, and invites us to follow in His footsteps (1 John 4:8-10). Where it is authentically practiced, flourishing and inclusive communities develop regardless of race or social status.

St Paul instructs us to **take every thought captive** and make it obey Christ (2 Corinthians 10:5). That means we need to analyse our thoughts and address those that do not align with what is taught by him. Just as we can learn to recognise his voice (John 10:27-28) we can learn to recognise the voice of the enemy of truth. We can learn to stop allowing ourselves to entertain destructive thoughts. It is a spiritual discipline we learn to exercise. Learning to defeat the enemy in our minds by refocusing on true and right thoughts (Philippians 4:8) is aided by being continuously filled with the Spirit.

For those significantly troubled by persistent negative thoughts, Cognitive Behavioural Therapy offers training in capturing thoughts, examining their validity, challenging negative thoughts, and creating more balanced beliefs. These skills can improve the debilitating symptoms of mood disorders. The teachings of Christ provide guidelines and standards that help us in recognizing thoughts that are debilitating and destructive to our wellbeing. Spiritual and cognitive therapies complement each other in the process of overcoming destructive thinking.

Thoughts that are often most troubling are the debilitating voices of condemnation that often plague our minds. St Paul says there is no condemnation for those who are in Christ Jesus (Romans 8:1) and when we are walking in step with the Spirit thoughts of condemnation are drowned out because we have learned to set our minds on what the Spirit desires.

The Spirit moves us to repentance and empowers us to change our way of thinking as we learn to refocus our thoughts on the goodness of our Heavenly Father and what His Son has done to free us from the powers of darkness. The Greek word used for power in relation to the Spirit is *dunamis* from which we get the word dynamite. In the battle against the powers of darkness we all encounter on a daily basis, we need the dynamism of the power of the Spirit.

Being filled with the Spirit

To be filled with the Holy Spirit involves a change of focus in our lives. It's something God wants to give us and something we need to want ourselves. St Paul said it's something we need to earnestly desire (1 Corinthians 14:1) and Jesus said will be given to anyone who is thirsty (John 7:37-39).

First, we need to get rid of the bitterness, hatred, and anger that grieves the Holy Spirit (Ephesians 4:30-31) and open up every part of our being to him. The Greek word used there for 'get rid of' literally means 'let it be removed'. In other words here we are letting it be taken away from us by leaving it at the cross of Christ that has freed us from its debilitating hold and empowered us to forgive as we have been forgiven.

We need to also throw away our idols and choose to speak and sing new songs of worship in our hearts and minds and on our lips as we are filled with the Spirit (Ephesians 5:19-20). That doesn't necessarily mean we sing because we feel great it means we speak and sing of the goodness of God **because of what God has done for us,** and we receive this by faith. Remember it's about praising God regardless of circumstances. Other gifts of the Spirit (I Corinthians 12) flow from this and are to be used to encourage others in their walk as well as for our edification.

Maintaining the fullness of the Spirit involves a battle of faith as we encounter subtle resistance to this new way of thinking and behaving. Despite having had our minds renewed we still battle against intrusive negative thoughts. As Bob Dylan once sang on his *Slow Train Coming* album "The enemy is subtle, howbeit we are deceived when the truth's in our hearts and we still don't believe". Deceptive spirits are active and they plot and plan to undermine faith.

CS Lewis describes this in his *Screwtape Letters*. He tells the story of a junior devil being instructed by a senior devil on how to undermine a new believer's faith by feeding negative thoughts. It is a daily battle everyone endures to some degree or other. Without well-developed spiritual disciplines, it is a very difficult battle indeed and can easily become overwhelming. Neil T Anderson has developed a series of steps to freedom we may find helpful particularly if we have had significant exposure to the dark side of the spiritual realm.

Mostly we are not very filled with the Spirit. Our flesh is often very much in control and we are hindered as we entertain unhelpful thoughts and allow ourselves to participate in dysfunctional behaviors. It need not be so if we are prepared to drown out the passions and desires of the flesh by living a life of worship and service to the King of Kings and Lord of Lords. We find this so magnificently expressed in classics such as Handel's Messiah, and so widely practised over many generations and cultures, and magnified during times of revival.

A regular quiet time

We need to make a regular time each day in a quiet place to worship, meditate on the Scriptures, take an inventory of what is happening in our lives, acknowledge our sins, forgive others, and pray for our world. This is much of what the Master taught when he was asked by the disciples as to how they should pray (Mathew 6:9-15).

In his *Study Guide* to *Celebration of Discipline,* Richard Foster makes the following observation about his experience of Biblical meditation.

> "Meditation is a more passive discipline. It is characterised more by reflecting than studying, more by listening than by thinking, and more by releasing than by grabbing. In the discipline of meditation, we are not so much acting as we are opening ourselves to be acted upon. We invite the Holy Spirit to come and work within us – teaching, cleansing, comforting, and rebuking. We also surround ourselves with the strong light of Christ to protect us from any influence not of God".

Meditation on the Word of God nourishes the primary way God speaks to us, inspiring us with his thoughts concerning our lives. They usually differ from our thoughts (Isaiah 55:8) and they are very different from the enemy's thoughts. In this regard, we need to learn the difference between thoughts of condemnation from the accuser and thoughts of conviction from the Holy Spirit.

Condemnation aims to trap us in a debilitating spiral of guilt and punishment from which we see no redemption. It may well come about because we ourselves are judging and condemning others (Romans 2:1). Conviction leads us to repentance (change) as we recognise that we have made choices incompatible with who we really are, acknowledge them before God, and ask for forgiveness.

We are cleansed from wrongdoing by the atonement Jesus made on the cross and freed to be able to make better choices in the future. The Holy Spirit is a comforter and counselor and we receive encouragement in our quiet times as we meditate on God's Word and apply it to our daily lives.

We are strengthened in our spirits as we learn to focus on what Christ has done rather than what we ought to be doing and we become more productive in our lives as we are empowered by the love of God to serve others rather than ourselves. We need to pray about our own issues and also for others in whatever battles they may be encountering in their journey, especially for leaders who carry significant responsibility.

It is good to begin each day by meditating on a few paragraphs of one of the books of the Bible. One way is to work your way through one of the four gospels Mathew, Mark,

Luke, or John. After that try going through one of the New Testament letters, then back to one of the gospels, then to a book of the Old Testament, then back to one of the gospels, etc. I've found that much more helpful than trying to go through the whole Bible from the beginning to the end, although it's good to do that at least once after a time to get a good overview of the sequence of historical events documented in its pages.

A good plan is to start with some worship songs, either with a musical instrument or by using recorded songs before your reading, and then have a time of prayer. The Lord's prayer (Mathew 5:9-13) provides a good outline to help us focus our prayers, as does 1 Timothy 2:1-2. Rather than just repeating the petitions we can ask for specific provisions, forgiveness for particular sins, grace to forgive those who have hurt us, and freedom from particular temptations. It's also good to end with praise and worship.

Practising the presence of God

As each day passes we can learn to live with an awareness of the presence of God in our lives. The risen Jesus promised to be always with his followers (Mathew 28:20). Practicing the presence of God involves acknowledging God's presence and learning to constantly surrender to him and become sensitive to what separates us from him. It means learning to resist useless and harmful thoughts and the behaviors they precipitate, but not becoming too mortified when we fail. When we fail we need to learn to acknowledge our failures before God as wrongdoing, ask for forgiveness and receive it by the grace of God.

When we do well in our actions of faith and love it's good to give thanks to God for his grace at work in us. The Master once said that apart from him we can't do anything (John 15:5) so there isn't a lot of room for us to become proud or boastful. If we succeed it is because we have been empowered to be successful, not because of our goodness but because of the gift we have been given. St Paul considered himself the chief of sinners despite all his achievements {1 Timothy 1:15) and we too need to remain aware of our sinfulness.

Living in the presence of God is the most joyful and rewarding life we can possibly live but that is not why we should want to experience it. We should do so because that is how God wants us to live, not to somehow earn salvation by living a good life, but because of what he has done for us and has created and equipped us to do (Ephesians 2:8-9). It is not something that is purely the domain of great saints, rather we can all live in conversation with God to some degree or the other. At the end of the day, our main business in life really is to learn to know God and live a life that is pleasing to God.

Life in the Spirit

What we usually spend most of our lives doing counts for nothing in the grand scheme of things if we are living according to our human nature (John 6:63). If we learn to live by the Spirit we can step off the meaningless treadmill of trying to gratify our flesh. Any success we think we may have with that usually doesn't last very long.

Living by the Spirit produces fruit that lasts. It doesn't mean we become so heavenly minded we are of no earthly good. Quite the opposite, it means that our lives become transformed as we respond to the call to participate in the

Great Commission of making disciples of all nations (Mathew 28:19-20), under the authority of Jesus and in whatever position or sphere we find ourselves in our communities.

The more individuals put this lifestyle into practice, the more families and communities are transformed. This was demonstrated by St Paul and the disciples of the first century and has continued to be throughout history since, as historian Tom Holland (Holland, 2019)[1] has recently documented. The change movement that began at Pentecost has transformed communities and nations since that time wherever it has spread.

The more we lose the practice of this Spirit-led lifestyle, the more the foundations of families, communities, and nations are eroded. In atheism, there is no basis for human rights or compassion for others, everything is permissible as Dostoyevsky once famously stated. The result is more of the heartbreaking consequences of disintegrating families. communities and nations at war with each other.

Our world is plagued by anxiety and fear as we continue to grasp at trying to define who we are and what we are here to be doing. Hatred, bullying, and prejudice thrive as long as we point the finger everywhere else rather than recognise what lies within our own hearts. We may well be surprised at what can happen in us, our families, and in our communities if we are willing to learn to regularly examine our hearts, turn away from fruitless activities, and live a life empowered by the Spirit.

---

1.   https://www.littlebrown.co.uk/little-brown-news/2023/05/04/read-an-extract-from-dominion-by-tom-holland/

Chapter Four
Transforming Communities

WE ALL NEED GOALS IN our lives to provide us with direction and help us work out our priorities. The Master provided a comprehensive goal for disciples to pursue that has resulted in the transformation of many communities and nations throughout the world. Nations that were once characterised by barbarism and tyranny became civilized, as attitudes towards racism, slavery, the role of women, the nurture of children in families, and the care of the poor began to change.

When pilgrims from many nations gathered together in Jerusalem to celebrate the day of Pentecost at the beginning of the first century a change movement that was to profoundly impact worldwide for generations to come, began with an outpouring of the Spirit. People from many nations in the known world heard a small group of uneducated Galilieans speaking of the wonders of God in their own language.

The sceptics said they were drunk. One of their leaders got up to speak and began by commenting that, as it was only nine o'clock in the morning, it was a bit too early for that. He went on to speak of events that had taken place in Jerusalem in the previous months that are still celebrated worldwide today. The sceptics that were present were outnumbered by some three thousand converts who responded to the message of Easter. Transformation of many communities across many nations was to come as followers spread the message that has endured to this day and continues to flourish, despite severe persecution in many nations.

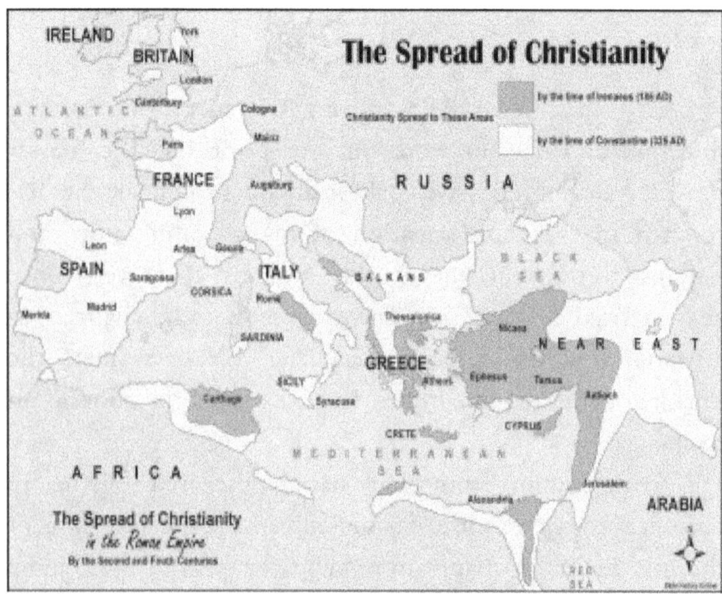

See Netchev, S. (2022). The Growth of Christianity in the Roman Empire[1]

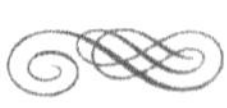

---

1. https://www.worldhistory.org/image/15640/the-growth-of-christianity-in-the-roman-empire/

TODAY WE CONVENE NUMEROUS national summits, conferences, and symposiums where experts are gathered to develop solutions to an ever-mounting list of social crises, but with little change to concerning trajectories. So **what can we learn from this enduring movement** that has positively impacted so many families, communities, and nations over so many centuries?

Power to facilitate change

The first thing to note is that we spend a lot of time debating what needs to change and coming up with statements and blueprints that articulate what we think needs to be done, but not much changes. Yes, we first need a change of heart but we also need to hear what the Master said to the disciples gathered in Jerusalem before his departure. He told them that repentance (change) and forgiveness of wrongdoing must be proclaimed in his name to all nations starting in Jerusalem, then in nearby regions, and then to the ends of the earth (Luke 24:47, Acts 1:8). He went on to say "But stay in the city until you are clothed with power from on high".

The power to facilitate change does not come from our own resources, though we do need to use them in the process. The power comes from the cross of Calvary through the agency of the Spirit and gives us the courage to say what needs to be said and do what needs to be done. That power came at Pentecost and is often released when followers of the way of the cross gather to pray before they act.

Not long after Pentecost, the disciples were confronted by city officials and told to stop talking about the resurrection that had happened in Jerusalem (Acts 4). Instead, they prayed for boldness to continue to speak and to heal, and that is exactly what happened as the Holy Spirit empowered them to proclaim the message of the cross and signs and wonders followed.

The courage to speak of the things they had heard and seen did not end with the twelve disciples who had spent three years with the Master. One of their chief opponents, a scribe and a scholar who was also a Roman citizen, encountered the risen Lord while on his way to arrest followers of the way in Damascus. He was so convinced by this encounter and the empowering of the Spirit that followed, that he went on to risk everything to proclaim the message to thousands of strangers despite the fact that they may well have considered what he had to say lunacy.

Saint Paul established congregations of believers across the known world as he proclaimed the God of love who was **willing to make himself nothing** and suffer a cruel death by crucifixion in order that we might be forgiven and freed from death. Many cities were transformed by the message, such that by 330 AD Christianity had become the belief of choice across the known world, despite attempts by a succession of tyrants and zealots to destroy its influence.

Many others have continued to proclaim the message in words and actions despite fierce opposition down through history to the present time. The change movement that began at Pentecost has renewed continually over the centuries. This has been seen in recent times in what Time magazine called the Jesus Revolution during the late sixties and seventies and it was seen in the revival that began at a university in the small Kentucky town of Asbury in 2023. The hallmark of this recent movement was young people experiencing a change of heart towards God and his purposes for their lives and taking time away from the socials to gather and sing Spirit-inspired songs of praise and worship, to pray, and to learn more of God's plan for their lives.

It is as our lives are turned around towards **loving God and one another** that we see pivotal changes in families, communities, and nations. It's not that summits, conferences, and royal commissions aren't important in assessing issues and developing strategies for change but they don't really address the issue of motivation and the capacity to do what is most needed. We need to keep going back to go back to Einstein's aphorism 'Science without religion is lame and religion without science is blind'. Science informs religion while religion provides spiritual resources to implement learnings from science.

The following graph illustrates the statistical increase in child protection notifications and, over the same period, the corresponding decrease in Christian affiliation as measured by the Australian Bureau of Statistics. No doubt there are many compounding factors involved but it does show that despite royal commissions and millions being poured into the sector, the escalation we are seeing in child abuse is not being contained as families continue to disintegrate and children increasingly suffer.

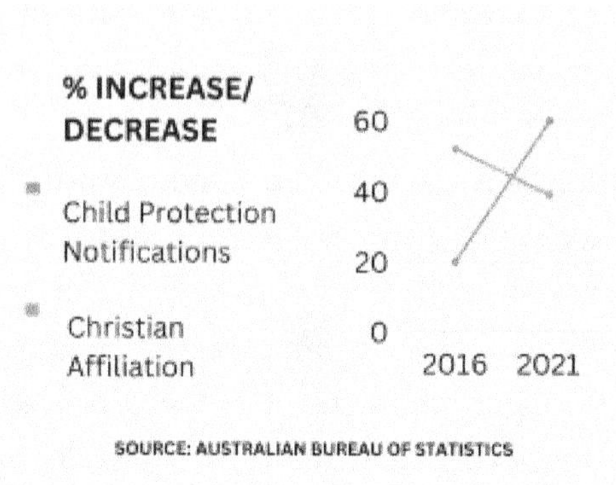

THE MISSING INGREDIENT of agape love

Without a change of heart through the agency of the Spirit the power of agape love that flows from such a pivot is a major missing ingredient in our efforts to change child welfare trajectories. Agape love is not the kind of whimsical human fantasy we often see portrayed in the many songs and sagas flaunted on our screens every day. It is a love that promotes the good of the person being loved aligned with the teachings of the Master (Tze Ming Ng et al, 2021). It distinguishes between good and evil, right and wrong, and runs counter to the popular narrative that champions the triumph of desire over the greater good. It is an endless, boundless love that can never be completely known, for God is love.

Agape love:

- turns the hearts of fathers, mothers, and carers toward caring for children.

· facilitates spiritual growth in others.

· motivates family support workers to offer the kind of love families really need if their hearts are to be softened.

· motivates leaders toward serving those under their responsibility rather than being heavy-handed.

· is an essential ingredient foundational in the development and practice of many transformative social initiatives.

· empowers leaders to stand for what is right in the face of slander, cancel culture, marginalisation, and victimisation.

· is a fruit of the Spirit at work in the hearts of believers.

Most of our lives lie somewhere between the selfless contributions of great saints and the misdemeanours of forgiven sinners. All great saints are flawed and God uses lowly sinners. The Master first called the twelve apostles to follow him and then sent out seventy disciples to proclaim the kingdom of God and to heal the sick. Some who were healed wanted to follow him but he sent them back to serve in their own communities.

Not all of us have the resilience to be the kind of radical disciples we see at work in the early church, especially if our lives have been severely traumatised as children, but we all can contribute toward the healing and transformation of our local communities. We need to remember that Jesus told his followers to make disciples of all nations (Mathew 28:19-20) and that implies that those of us who are able, are needed to participate in this challenge in whatever local, national, or international sphere of influence we find ourselves.

The agency of the Spirit

As politically correct populists seek to eliminate prayers from their opening agendas and limit our capacity to mere thoughts, the reality is that we can not do a lot in our own strength. If we are to see the agency of the Spirit at work we need to first ASK (Luke 11:11-13). The spontaneous prayer meeting at Asbury in 2023 that went on for two weeks ended up being attended by thousands from all over the world who spread it into their communities. The Moravians started a 24/7 prayer meeting in 1727 that lasted for a century. Prayer has always been the hallmark of renewal and revival that has led to significant spiritual and social change.

Prayer includes both talking and listening. As well as asking things of God each of us needs to learn to listen for guidance and direction regarding the part we are to play in bringing about transformation. We can do this individually, in twos or threes or we can do it corporately with larger groups. With the Spirit's inspiration, we can receive specific directions to help formulate plans to facilitate change in families and communities. It is these inspired plans that bring lasting change. We need to be intentional about spiritual as well as scientific research in our planning and include spiritual resources in implementing strategies for change.

Receiving guidance in decision-making can be a challenging exercise. These are some pivotal considerations. The first one is that **our heart needs to be in what we are planning** to commit to doing. If it is not our motivation will wane and we will struggle to stay the course. The second is that the **circumstances** and the timing need to be right. The third and probably most challenging one is that we need to hear a reasonably **clear direction from God** that confirms the decision we are to make. That may take many forms but suffice it to say the Spirit of God communicates with our spirit in a variety of ways.

How does the Spirit do this? Martin Luther once wrote a letter to his barber in response to a question about how he prayed. In it, he said that "It often happens that I lose myself in such rich thoughts (literally that 'my thoughts go for a walk'). When such rich thoughts come, one should let the other prayers go and give room to these thoughts, listen to them in silence, and by no means suppress them. For here the Holy Spirit himself is preaching and one word of his sermon is better than thousands of our own prayers".

The Spirit may communicate with our spirit through such rich thoughts. Other means of receiving guidance may include timely words of Scripture, impressions, visions, dreams, etc. We can readily find examples of all of these in both the Old and New Testaments and also down through history since then. Discernment is needed which is why the two other considerations we have mentioned are important. A sense of peace usually follows the decision and if it doesn't we need to reconsider (see Philippians 4:7, Colossians 3:15). Sometimes the Spirit can simply close a door and prevent us from doing something such as we see in the Book of Acts when Paul tried to enter Bithynia (Acts 16:7).

Governance and partnerships

It is one thing to be led by the Spirit as individuals and another as a community. As renewed individuals continue the daily battle with the flesh, so it is with renewed communities. After Pentecost, the early believers began to meet together regularly for teaching, worship, and prayer. They also began to share their possessions with those among them in need. Daily distribution of food to widows was an issue that became a challenge for their leaders, so they asked the Jerusalem community to appoint seven deacons to take responsibility for this so that they could continue to devote themselves primarily to prayer and teaching the Word of God (Acts 6:1-4).

When Paul established new communities in other cities he, along with Barnabas, appointed elders, choosing wisely after prayer and fasting (Acts 14:21-23). Meanwhile, the apostles and elders in Jerusalem formed a council to deal with issues that arose there, as well as in the rapidly expanding broader church (Acts 15). As evangelists continued to go out to spread the message of the kingdom of God, apostles continued to establish governance in the new communities, pastors and teachers helped them grow in faith and action, while prophets spoke out against injustice and warned of what was to come when communities and nations were crumbling on eroding foundations.

The early church was a radical, counter-cultural gathering of believers who, against all odds and empowered by the Spirit, transformed cities and nations and set a pattern for future generations. Where that pattern has been followed and well translated into the language and culture of the times, the church has thrived and communities and nations have been positively impacted. Where it has waned communities and nations have descended into moral decay and social disintegration, often followed by autocratic rule as nations strive to rise from the ashes.

That is not to say all is well wherever the church has been operative. The Greek word for church is *ekklesia* which was originally a term used for the Greek governing body assembled to govern their city-states. It was later adapted by the Romans and was a well-known term to Jesus and the general public at that time (Silvoso, 2017). He adapted it further, incorporating small gatherings of two or three in His presence (Mathew 18:20) as well as large assemblies. Nevertheless, it was a governing body capable of curating the transformation of cities and nations and demolishing the crime-ridden hell many communities experience (Mathew 16:18).

Where the *Ekklesia* is corrupted by fleshly operators who have become more concerned about their own interests than the good of their communities, damaging exploitation results. Where it has operated among those with clean hearts, renewed spirits, and transformed minds, lives have been changed for the better and communities have been renewed through spiritual and social change. When prayer flourishes the Spirit flows and community transformation begins to take place as broken lives are restored and we see change-makers work together on community initiatives that have a collective impact.

Communities, municipalities, and nations that are looking solely to secular local and national governments for community transformation are bound to end up disappointed.

The Master and the early apostles respected the role of secular government and encouraged the early believers to pray for it and to be tax-paying, cooperative citizens (Luke 20:20-26, Romans 13). The concept of *ekklesia* however also included the agency of the Holy Spirit, producing agape love in the lives of believers and their communities in response to agreement in prayer.

Significant community transformation has occurred when faith communities have partnered with governments and other community groups in working together for change. When churches become too spiritual and isolated from local communities harmful sectarian tendencies can develop, and when governments begin to think they can do it all alone they are usually frustrated when it comes to delivering pivotal change. By partnering together, with some understood boundaries and informed policies in place, they can collectively impact a lot more citizens and their communities for good.

The best approach to dealing with **intergenerational trauma** is to prevent it from happening in the first place. Mothers, fathers, husbands, and wives all need to be able to fulfil their roles in nurturing babies, raising children, and training them to be able to repeat the process. Transforming cycles of intergenerational trauma into intergenerational cycles of nurturing and recovery is a long-term process. That is not to say government initiatives in social services and education can't help a lot when we are dealing with entrenched social disadvantage, but at the end of the day, the contribution of informed parental nurture and care is critical.

We need to put a lot more focus on investing in parenting in families. When governments work well together with local families and communities, adding value to existing assets, significant progress toward community transformation can occur. That is not to say there aren't any **creative tensions** in the process, but they do need each other if we are to see extensive community and national transformation.

For example, much of the 'woke' agenda as well as much of the conservative agenda can be traced back to Christian values. Too much alignment among churches with either side of the party-political spectrum imposes significant limitations on the change process. The *Ekklesia* needs to provide ethical and moral leadership in relation to who is elected as local representatives, and with regard to specific legislation that comes before Parliament. Elected representatives are mostly bound to party policies and need a lot of prayer and elector support in relation to some of the more challenging items on the legislative agenda if they beg to differ.

Churches can easily become too politically aligned to the left or to the right and governments can overreach their mandate into areas better left to the *Ekklesia*. We are currently seeing something of an epidemic of both and the resulting prognosis for our communities isn't good. Hopefully, the church can steward the current faith revival among young people better than it has previously, and governments can stop entertaining attempts to marginalise the *Ekklesia* by restricting its freedom to address the challenge of standing against the scourge of wrongdoing.

A sick society needs to be healed in heart, mind, body, and spirit, in the same manner as individuals need to be healed. As levels of anxiety, disintegration, and fear escalate and unhealthy practices and policies emerge, it is good for all of us, whether serving in church or state, to become more prayerful and willing to pivot in order to facilitate change. The promise of 2 Chronicles 7:14 is that when we humble ourselves, turn away from evil, and pray we will receive forgiveness and healing in our land.

Community transformation

Revival of faith has never resulted in utopian communities though there have been some notable examples of significant community renewal, at least for a time. It was said of the early church that there was not a needy person among them. Those with plenty and those with little shared their resources with those in need (Acts 2:44-45). They regularly broke bread in their homes and met together in the temple courts to worship God. Signs and wonders, including healings, occurred and their numbers increased daily. As time went by however issues emerged that undermined some of the outcomes of the earlier days and uncovered the fragility of the relationships involved in the New Testament communities.

If we take a cursory look at history we find a revolving pattern continuing among faith communities to the present time. Over the centuries, Christianity expanded across Europe and established significant influence across secular institutions. **A pattern of decline and revival** occurred in which the Catholic church became corrupted and then renewed with the emergence of monastic community movements such as the Franciscans. Most of these still survive today and new expressions continue to emerge such as the Evangelical Sisterhood of Mary[2] that was built at Darmstadt in Germany on daily repentance (Schlink, 1959), literally out of the ruins

---

2.   https://en.kanaan.org/

of the second world war, and has since spread to a number of other nations.

By the 16th century, entrenched corruption was such that radical reformation was needed to change the practices of the old order, and new Protestant churches emerged as a result. They too followed the same pattern and regularly regressed into staid institutionalism and were in need of renewal and revival. One such revival occurred among the Moravians who congregated at Count von Zinzendorf's Herrnhut estate in Germany in the early eighteenth century. It had a profound worldwide influence in the years that followed.

One of the many impacted by their spirituality and agape love was John Wesley the founder of the Methodist movement which spread across Europe and America. A pivotal event occurred on May 24th, 1738, when Wesley's heart was 'strangely warmed' when a passage from Martin Luther's *Preface to Romans* was being read. He became empowered by Holy Spirit *dunamis* to spread the Word of God as he traversed England and established faith gatherings which eventually became the Methodist Church.

The 24/7 prayer movement initiated at Herrnhut that lasted one hundred years may have waned for a time but it has been revived again in recent decades. Prayer meetings have extended over several years in intercession for the nations. The Order of the Mustard Seed founded by the Moravians, committing its adherents to spread the message with agape love shown through acts of kindness, is also being revived. Songs that came out of this movement including the many hymns of Charles Wesley, John's brother, are still widely used today.

In the nineteenth century, the Wesleyan movement with its innovative classes for discipleship, fellowship, and pastoral care began to spread. Methodists were also very active in supporting oppressed workers as well as engaging in prayer and vibrant hymn singing. As happened in many similar movements, such as the Presbyterianism that emerged in Scotland at around the same time, they soon became staid, more respectable denominations over time. However, some of their influences remain. The roots of the recent revival emerging from Asbury University can be traced back to the Wesleyan movement. The university was named after Francis Asbury, the major figure in the founding of American Methodism.

William Booth, the founder of the Salvation Army, was an ordained Wesleyan. The Army was formed when the Booths left the institutionalising Methodist church in 1865 and took to the streets with social action and brass bands, reaching the hearts of the masses in the later part of the nineteenth century. Its military slant was epitomised in the still-published *War Cry* magazine. It has spread across the world and is well known for its social work in caring for the poor and dispossessed and still considers itself to be a movement, though it too has become somewhat institutionalised.

The beginning of the twentieth century saw the emergence of the Pentecostal movement which has become the fastest-growing church expression worldwide today. The movement has brought about a refocus on the sometimes neglected third person of the Trinity, the work of the Holy Spirit. It influenced the charismatic renewal that took place in mainstream churches in the latter part of the 20th century.

Many congregations were renewed and became more vibrant communities, despite intense resistance from some institutional church hierarchies.

The sixties and seventies were a time of great upheaval among young people as many turned away from the values of previous generations and turned to hallucinogenic drugs, mysticism, and the occult in their search for God. Many of them encountered the reality of the Holy Spirit in their lives when what became known as the Jesus Revolution[3] began to take hold in many countries worldwide. Para-churches emerged and some traditional churches that embraced new expressions of worship and community development flourished. In at least one instance, at Calvary Chapel in Los Angeles, that happened very quickly, while in other settings change emerged over several decades.

In attempting to rehabilitate often very broken lives community houses were set up with names like Agape House to accommodate growing numbers of often addicted and traumatised young people in need of a haven (Sparks, 1974, Olsen, 2020). Needless to say, most were relatively short-lived, given the enormous challenges they faced. At least one initiative founded by David Wilkerson in the streets of New York City in the sixties has survived to the present day, with thousands of rehab centres established in some 129 countries. It has operated successfully mostly without government funding and with a focus on the spiritual growth of participants, as well as the social emotional, and cognitive elements in the programs.

---

3.   https://jesusrevolution.movie/

In recent decades Christianity has also seen a remarkable expansion in countries such as China, Africa, and South America, preceded by the work of self-sacrificing, adventurous missionaries who spread the message of the cross with acts of agape love and translation of the good news into indigenous languages. What the missionaries were used to begin has been taken up by spirit-filled locals and has spread across continents. Many of the countries involved have also experienced **strong economic and social benefits**, paralleling the development of faith communities across their regions.

After seventeen years of intense persecution under a Marxist regime ending in 1991, Ethiopia saw a revival break out mainly among students who then took up appointments across the country, and spread the message. The Ethiopian Evangelical Church Mekane Yesus claimed almost 2.3 million members in 2007 and grew to 8.3 million baptized members according to the 2016 statistics. In the decade before 2016, the Ethiopian GDP grew at a rate between 8% and 11% annually – one of the fastest-growing states among the 188 IMF member countries. South Korea saw a similar pattern a few decades earlier. South Korea's economy was one of the world's fastest-growing from the early 1960s to the late 1990s. In 1970 its population was eighteen percent Christian and by 2000 it had grown to thirty-one percent.

The nation of Israel is also an instructive case in point. It saw great economic growth when King David re-established its foundations and territory and his son Solomon built the temple in Jerusalem in 950 BC. Its prosperity fluctuated under kings of varying persuasions until its decline was such that the Babylonians captured it 363 years later when the Jews were exiled to Babylon and the temple was destroyed. It was rebuilt seventy years later when Persian King Cyrus allowed the Jews to return to Israel but was burned by Roman armies in 70 AD when the Jews were deported as slaves across the Roman empire.

The Jewish people remained in exile for nearly 2,000 years until Israel was reestablished in 1947 after the horrors of the Holocaust contributed to the will of the international community to support its rebirth. When the Jews turned toward God they were blessed and when they turned away from God they suffered enormously. The transformation of once desolate land to the fertile plains and thriving nation of today has been remarkable but it remains to be seen how the future of this pivotal nation, its rebirth prop[hesied[4] thousands of years ago and surrounded by enemy states, will eventuate. Will those who live in Jerusalem hear the voice of the prophets and turn to the Messiah who has come and promises to come again?

4.	https://www.icej.org/understand-israel/biblical-teachings/the-restoration-of-israel/

Photo: Screenshot via Harvest Journeys/Youtube[5]

TODAY YOU CAN TRAVEL to the geographical heart of Australia and see a giant, 20-metre cross on the top of Memory Mountain, 230k west of Alice Springs. It came out of a vision given to a local elder, Nebo Jugadai, at an Easter celebration one night at the foot of the mountain, and was first proposed by local residents in 2009 before being completed, after overcoming many hurdles, in 2023. The Forgiveness Cross stands as a reflection of the impact of the message of the cross on many Aboriginal communities and sign of hope for the present time.

It has been built as a meeting place for prayer and worship where everyone is welcome. Memory Mountain was named in honor of four indigenous missionaries who brought the message of the cross to the region in 1923. At the geographical

5. https://www.youtube.com/watch?v=iv5zrL_bp-w

heart of Australia Aboriginal and white people regularly gather for praise and worship singalongs, especially at Easter. The locals often gather nightly to worship the One who has brought forgiveness and healing to many and to pray for revival among the nations.

When missionaries began to hand over leadership to local pastors and evangelists in the 1970s revival broke out as indigenous people began to use the gifts of preaching, teaching, healing, songwriting, and singing. On Elcho Island, off the coast of Arnhem Land in the Northern Territory, some locals had been praying for three years when in 1979 God's Spirit began to move. Many experienced healing as people began to pray, sing songs of praise and worship, and spread the message of the cross.

In the power of the Spirit, they went south through the Northern Territory and into Western Australia and South Australia. Such was the impact that the Warburton Ranges, described by the then Minister for Aboriginal Affairs as the worst place in Australia, had now become a happy place. Many locals were set free from fear and the scourge of alcohol. Rev Dr. Djininynini Gondarra reported that a nursing sister had told him that during one week no one went to the local hospital (Hart,1988, p37).

Clearly, though, it must be said, the campfire needs to be kept burning or it will die out. Having experienced spiritual renewal many still have underlying longer-term issues to deal with such as the intergenerational trauma lying at the root of many of the social challenges in local communities. Ongoing discipling, counseling, pastoral care, and rehab are often needed in communities renewed by the Spirit in order to consolidate breakthroughs in the lives of individuals.

Most communities struggle to maintain the level of support required for individuals and families who have been traumatised over many generations. Supporting new parents to nurture and care for their children is particularly needed. The first few years are critical for child development and parents need to be prepared for the challenges they experience in caring for babies and toddlers. They need support from extended family, if that is available, as well as other early years services. Family hubs with a focus on supporting parenting are particularly beneficial for parents who themselves have been traumatized in their own early years.

Renewal, revival, and reformation can be messy as entrenched patterns of dysfunctional behavior are challenged. Not everyone goes with the flow and major disruptions to family and community life can be precipitated. Much wisdom from those in positions of authority in the communities involved is required, as is the relinquishment of strongly held but counterproductive traditions. Overall the long-term benefits usually far outweigh the challenges and radical humility is needed by all in the process of change if trajectories of decline are to pivot.

The early church had a strong **social agenda** as well as a spiritual one. Key areas of social activity included addressing systemic poverty, slavery, the status of women, and restoring families. As well as giving to the poor, productivity in terms of those receiving benefits giving back to the community was encouraged (Ephesians 4:28).

While poverty was addressed almost immediately in their communities, it took until the nineteenth century for slavery to be eventually abolished when William Wilberforce took up the final battle in the British Parliament. The demeaning status of women was challenged by advocating for the equality of women with men (Galatians 3:28). That battle has also continued through history as has the challenge of disadvantaged communities in restoring family functionality and empowering families to raise secure and healthy children.

In the Book of Exodus we see God promised to show "love to thousands of generations of those who love me and keep my commandments" (Exodus 20:6). The source of the kind of agape love that we all need is our Maker and Redeemer, but we all have a lot of trouble trying to keep the commandments by our own efforts. We do a lot better when we understand that the curse of sin has been broken on the sacrificial cross of Christ and freed us to love and care for our children and their communities. The power to do that in the manner our Maker intended comes to us through the cross by the Spirit given to those who ask (Luke 11:11-13). It lies at the heart of the kind of community transformation that has a sustainable collective impact.

Community and AI technology

If we believe that science is going to provide us with all the answers to the problems we face we are bound to be disappointed. The optimism of inevitable progress through science advancing humankind is on very shaky ground, as recent history suggests. An increasing trajectory of child abuse, family breakdown, global warming, war, pandemics, and crime is not progress. At the heart of it, lies our relentless pursuit of self-interest, and if we incrementally hand over decisions to artificial intelligence for solutions, we are dealing with the possibility of unprecedented global tyranny with social control at the core.

In many ways, the current fragmentation in many communities has come about because we cannot agree on the most basic ideas of what human nature is like and what it is to flourish. The optimistic Enlightenment idea that we are all basically good and can get along better without putting out trust in God has not produced the utopia some prominent nineteenth-century thinkers imagined.

Atheistic humanism sprouted both Communism and Naziism and the horrific atrocities that followed. Before the rise of Marxism and Social Darwinism many national leaders looked to a higher authority in making decisions about the validity of such monumental issues as going to war or less significant legislative change. When **absolute political power** is acquired by autocratic leaders who do not contemplate their accountability to any such authority, there are usually concerning consequences that follow.

That is why Tolkien's publishing and cinematic phenomenon *Lord of the Rings* penned the resonating narrative that such power must not fall into the hands of evil megalomaniacs. In the ultimate battle between good and evil, if a nuclear world war eventuates, global warming destroys the earth, pandemics wipe out huge populations, or if we succumb to algorithms constructed by malevolent despots, the return of the King is our only real avenue of hope (Zechariah 14, Revelation 19:11-21). What was once considered fantasy is rapidly becoming a stark possibility.

Added to the dangers of too much power resting in the hands of rudderless autocrats, we now have the concern of what **Artificial General Intelligence** might have in store for us. We are already seeing extensive social control through AI technology being implemented in countries such as China with its social credit system. If you are caught associating with an 'unsafe person' by any of its over 4 million CCTV surveillance cameras' facial recognition techniques you may end up being labeled as a 'discredited person' on a public television screen as you walk past. While this technology can be very helpful in fighting crime, it can also be used to counter any change movement that presents a challenge to those wanting to hold on to dictatorial power.

The internet is controlling information in a way we could never have imagined. Most of us have no idea about what is going on. We are seeing international hackers creating mayhem using AI to hack companies with large data banks and posting personal information on the dark web. What is more concerning however is the possibility of implants creating an interface between technology and humans which would make human beings essentially hackable as well.

Many dream of a new world of transhumanism where cyber technology enhances not just human existence but humans themselves. The idea of humans merging with technology is being explored by some leading scientists with aspirations to re-engineer humans into superhumans. Such humans would potentially have the capacity to hack other humans and eventually take over humankind. What was once science fiction is rapidly becoming a distinct possibility.

While many benefits, including social connection and enormous information accessibility, have come from information technology it has also become a haven for cybercriminals to manipulate and extort from large enterprises, as well as for smaller operators to deceive and prey on the vulnerable. As well as providing obvious benefits, technology has provided platforms with a capability for apocalyptic evil that was considered unimaginable only a few short years ago.

It is the attempts to develop unregulated super intelligence by powerful operators with extensive worldwide influence that is of greatest concern. Relegating critical decision-making to the machinations of powerful computer algorithms has now become a threat to our very future. **Self-programming** AI is not a way-off scenario, it is at our window. Generative AI is already causing an ethical conundrum but AGI will create ethical dilemmas of literally Biblical proportions. It is the capacity of AI systems to out-think the human race that is of real concern.

Many scientists in the field, including Geoffrey Hinton, Max Tegmark, Sam Altman, and other notable AI developers, have warned us of the threat of extinction[6] from AGI. High-tech company executives, such as Elon Musk and Steve Wozniak, and other luminaries suggest that we put a pause on research[7] into 'human competitive' intelligence as well-resourced tech companies attempt to outmanoeuver each other in creating what could be described as a digital God that may be politically attractive and financially lucrative but

---

6.   https://www.safe.ai/statement-on-ai-risk

7.   https://futureoflife.org/open-letter/pause-giant-ai-experiments/

is untruthful. From what we have observed about the human heart we can predict that such a pause is unlikely to happen.

An elite few have made billions from their platforms and products by developing sophisticated algorithms to capture huge markets. They have accumulated so much wealth and computing power that they are now in a position to disproportionately influence decision-makers and policymakers with Godlike pronouncements and media control. They have commanded so much influence that they will find it very difficult to surrender to the actual God and more easily opt to give control to the algorithms instead.

That is not as big a step today as we might once have imagined. According to Geoffrey Hinton who is also a cognitive psychologist, Generative AI can already outperform the human brain and the potential for manipulation of large numbers in the hands of malevolent operators propagating tailored misinformation is frightening. Even the developers don't know the full capability of what they are developing. The impressive nature of machine learning's ability to outperform the human brain will no doubt influence many to follow its untrustworthy dictates. This becomes particularly alarming when it falls into the manipulative hands of unethical operators.

Hinton used his understanding of neural networks to develop machine learning using a Forward Forward algorithm[8] to process data that could be generated solely by the network. He is now raising concerns about how factors such as competition with other companies for the search business are driving them away from the once-responsible development of

---

8.   https://www.cs.toronto.edu/~hinton/FFA13.pdf

AI. This development led him to resign from his company position in order to be able to speak more freely about these concerns and advocate for urgent regulation.

Who exactly is in a position to regulate the global phenomenon of AGI? Individual governments? The United Nations? The OECD? The EU? The G20? The G7? Responsible national governments may attempt to legislate ethical regulations but what about irresponsible autocratic regimes? Will they then gain the upper hand and use AGI to control the global community? It's not too difficult to see a move for a one world government on the near horizon. From what we know about too much power concentrated in the hands of too few that is also a very frightening scenario (Revelation 13:7-8).

Autonomous super-intelligent machines that influence our moral choices will not lead us toward God and a gloriously painless future. Rather they will lead to the greatest rejection of God the world has ever seen (Lennox, 2020), and the unmitigated evil of hardened hearts are very likely to follow. Like nuclear physics, AGI can be used for good and it can be used for evil. It can help connect communities and inform families online and it could disintegrate communities and disrupt and destroy life as we have known it.

AI is poised to dominate our lives including our **relationships** and will lead to the disintegration of communities if it cannot be well regulated and that is not likely given the current challenges of regulating social media, as well as what we know of the human heart. Much of social media has become a haven for bullying, abuse, and extortion and regulators are very challenged in finding ways to contain it.

Some experts suggest we can regulate AI until it is smarter than us and it already is smarter than us.

Alongside the impact of the toxic side of social media in our lives, some, in fact, are looking to relationships with robots to meet their need for affirmation and fulfilment. Despite the robotic capacity to express feelings, that is a very hollow kind of relationship when deep down we know it will lead us to live in a fantasy world lacking real empathy and compassion toward real people. Becoming accustomed to treating other people like machines who exist for our self-gratification, is not likely to lead to healthy relationships.

We can not find another way of getting around the problem of human sin, greed, and the destructive exercise of illegitimate power. The only real solution to the problem of sin and selfishness has been provided by Jesus Christ who dealt with it once and for all by giving his life on the cross of Calvary and making forgiveness and the power to change available to all (2 Corinthians 5:15).

As wrongdoing and evil proliferate, we do well to take seriously the prophetic words of Christ and the prophets of the Old and New Testaments in relation to our current challenges. The scourge of inter-generational trauma continues to perpetuate as families and communities struggle to raise children to become good citizens. As hearts become hardened and consciences are seared trauma and terror are perpetuated. It happens with individuals and it happens with communities and nations.

We all have an innate longing for another more enduring world. That is what drives much of the development of transhumanism. The pursuit of that dream could destroy our communities if we are taken over by mindless technology or it can lead us to an evidence-based trust in the God who wants to gift us with the eternal life we all long to have.

A faith-integrated approach

Our world is in considerable trouble and the anxiety many are experiencing because of it is not unfounded. The main problem is we all tend to want to make ourselves comfortable and go with the flow of what we think is needed to achieve that and ignore actively engaging with the battle in our hearts and minds that continues each day. It is true for leaders whose access to power corrupts, and whose absolute power corrupts absolutely, as it is true for all individuals.

Our human craving for recognition and influence is unsatiable and we so easily ignore justice and walk over others in pursuit of our self-centred ambitions. Repentance is needed on a regular basis, as is being continuously filled with the Spirit. Only then do we see the agape love we all need at work among us, neutralising fear and transforming broken lives.

The founders of many of our institutions included prayer in their agendas before decisions were made for a very good reason. Rather than banning it, we need a lot more of it, if we are going to see significant change in terms of community transformation. The Master told us to watch and pray so that we do not fall into temptation (Luke 22:46) and there are plenty of those on offer to distract us from the goal of seeing families, communities, and nations become transformed.

More than ever we need a faith-integrated approach to underpin our understanding of the various domains impacting communities. Science, social services, psychology, counseling, higher education, politics, environment, media, entertainment, leadership, and technology all need to be part of the conversation. Each discipline impacts the other as they are part of a complex system, and we need followers of the Way to be contributing to the conversations going on in each of them.

We also need a more informed holistic understanding of how the dynamics of **power and love** have impacted communities in the past and how they can impact the present challenges of families and communities (Kahane, 2018). Both are important and both need to be kept in balance with each other (1 Corinthians 13). Martin Luther King captured this well with his aphorism, "Power without love is reckless and abusive, and love without power is sentimental and anemic".

Changemakers need to be empowered and authorised to facilitate change and we need love to build and maintain connection with each other. When we choose one at the expense of the other we end up with either immoral power or powerless moralism. It is a conflict within us as individuals, as it is within communities, and we see it playing out every day.

The kind of both power and love Christ offers us through his Spirit equips us to find a way through the complex problems we face. We can find healing among fractured communities by regularly consulting with the One who has broken down the dividing wall of conflict between people of different cultures and persuasions (Ephesians 2:14-18). He can prevent us from the extremes of being reckless and abusive or sentimental and anemic and empower us to be reconciled with each other and be agents of transformation.

According to the Scriptures, our struggle is not primarily against individuals but against **principalities and powers** that militate against community transformation (Ephesians 6:12).

That the power that will ultimately triumph came from what happened on a cross on a hill in Israel two thousand years ago is inconceivable to human minds. It operates above party politics and autocratic dictatorships and is stewarded through the prayers and actions of believers accountable to a higher power.

Where other religions have advanced through the power of the sword and/or population growth safeguarded by strict anti-conversion laws, Christianity has advanced through the proclamation of what happened on a cross and the signs and wonders confirming the message that followed. It is sustained in communities over long periods with the support of leaders in government who also follow in the footsteps of the Master (Acts 18:9-11, Romans 16:23).

St Paul's account that Christ said to him "My grace is sufficient for you for my power is made perfect in weakness" (2 Corinthians 13:9) remains a mystery to those who seek to rule by the exercise of tyrannical power, yet the power of sacrificial agape love continues to ultimately triumph among a conflicted humanity. Hitler, among others influenced by the powers of darkness, some more prominent than others, despised this kind of power as he became more and more aligned with evil.

Power made perfect in weakness is exercised by leaders who understand their own weaknesses and the futility of attempting to ruthlessly dominate others. **Servant leadership** is a hallmark of their service as they endeavour to build communities by connecting people to work together through extensive networking. They do not look for credit for what they do and understand that a lot more can be achieved when we don't mind who gets the credit.

Servant leaders are able to give the abuse and mistreatment they encounter over to the God they serve and continue to act in love rather than out of bitterness. The authority they exercise derives not only from their position but also from a prayerful walk as they live in the understanding that we are all dependent on the grace of God if anything of lasting value is to be achieved.

We saw something of the significance of this kind of authority in the anointing of Charles 111 as king which was not meant to simply be an archaic ritual from another era but an actual impartation of the Holy Spirit for sacrificial servant leadership. Sadly much of the meaning of the coronation event was obscured by the excessive, dated pageantry, language, and culture of the past. Too many churches are caught up in traditions that need to be translated into today's language and culture, without changing the original intent and meaning of their practices.

Jesus did not come to be served but to serve and to give his life as a ransom for many (Mathew 20:28). Servant leadership is demanding and leaders need a lot of prayer for the empowering of the Holy Spirit to meet the challenges of serving the communities they represent. Faith and prayer were clearly a source of great strength for Queen Elizabeth 11, as she often expressed more openly in her later years. Everyone in a position of leadership needs much wisdom, courage, and grace if they are to responsibly and justly serve as leaders.

Mega churches that have too much centralised power can easily fall into the same pitfalls as can large denominations. Temptations to abuse power are magnified among leaders in top-down structures with too much power concentrated at the top of the hierarchy. Leaders can be made less susceptible when organisations distribute decision-making power. The same could be said of attempts to form a centralised one-world government. The potential for the abuse of power in that scenario would be astronomical.

In churches, it is better to develop more decentralised structures less prone to corruption by establishing **bottom-up decision-making processes**, while still being authorised to exercise appropriate supervision of leaders. Team leaders need to be able to make decisions with their ministry teams in relation to their agreed mission plans without too much unnecessary top-down interference. There are times when leaders in the field need to be able to make a captain's call if the team is to be successful. That also enables communities to develop more organically, freer from bureaucratic control, and more open to the leading of the Spirit, as we saw happening in the early church.

History documents the ongoing battles between the opposing forces of good and evil. The ultimate triumph of agape love over evil is yet to be fully revealed. In this chapter, we have looked at some elements and outcomes of a movement that has been transformational in many communities and nations over the past two thousand years. Christianity is still the world's largest religion with some 30% of the population adhering to its message and its values (Blainey, 2011). Other faiths share some of the same values but the evidence of history suggests the Spirit of Christ remains the most powerful change agent for good, in a world of changing hearts and changing communities.

Christianity has produced some notable failures such as the medieval Crusades provoked by the destruction of sacred sites in Jerusalem and the more recent sexual abuse by some of the clergy, but in the main, the benefits have far outweighed the failures. No other movement has ever gone near to replicating the kind of community transformation initiated by the One who sacrificed his life in order that we might have life.

The transformative message of the cross lies at the heart of civilization as we know it, despite intense persecution and continued attempts to cancel out its influence. Community transformation happens most powerfully when believers learn to live out their lives daily in the presence of God and take care of the disadvantaged and vulnerable. Sometimes that presence is quite tangible such as during times of Spirit-anointed worship. Mostly, however, we need to anchor our lives in the facts and live by faith rather than be ruled by feelings, as we encounter the challenges of life.

Jesus instructed his disciples to worship in **spirit and in truth** (John 4:23-24) and both elements are needed to keep us on track. In an age of moral relativism, too few know what to believe and we need to be very careful about falling into accommodating what we know on a more thorough analysis not to be true. We can easily do this when we do not fully understand the complexity of the whole picture and succumb to what may appear to be correct at first glance but has disturbing consequences in the longer term. Only God fully understands each aspect of the entire system that is in operation and that is why we need to continually take off our reductionist blinkers and take a knee to the Creator in our decision making.

Applying spiritual disciplines involved in practicing the presence of God and continuing to walk by faith helps us negotiate both the trials and the triumphs of life. In the final analysis, we can say that the more our hearts become hardened against God and we believe we can do whatever we like with impunity, the more we end up with the evil that proliferates in disintegrating communities. On the other hand, the more we turn away from wrongdoing, and invite God to change our hearts, the more we become empowered by the Spirit to be renewed in heart and mind, and the more we see communities and nations being transformed.

Chapter Five
What can we do?

If statistics are showing us the trajectory of child abuse and neglect has been consistently escalating in recent decades then we need to ask why our families and children once actually did better. In nations where we are seeing a decline in the practice of Judeo-Christian values in families and communities, we are seeing a parallel increase in a mental health crisis among adults and children. In the current environment, child abuse and neglect are escalating as our child protection systems become increasingly overwhelmed, despite royal commissions, inquiries, and money being pumped into attempts to shore up gaps in the system.

Broken communities, many being terrorized by uncontrolled gangs of drunken teenagers roaming the streets, starting fights, stealing cars and breaking into houses, are crying out for more policing, more money to fight crime, and stricter laws such as bans on alcohol and implementation of curfews.

Cries for crisis intervention often only scratch the surface as we are usually dealing with the impacts of intergenerational trauma that simmers in the hearts and minds of both the perpetrators and the victims involved. Some, who often themselves grew up in violent homes, use violence as a means of venting their troubled souls or turn to drugs and alcohol to deaden their emotional pain. Others attempt to redefine their identity in the hope that they will find relief from inner turmoil and belong to a community that will support them and protects them from being abused and bullied.

Finding security

The insecurity that is bred in the hearts and minds of children growing up in a trauma-filled environment is very difficult to heal. What has been wired into the brain in the early years is very difficult to change in adulthood. It takes a lot more than policing, money, stricter laws, and louder voices in parliament to pivot communities in turmoil. A change of heart is needed across whole communities if we are to see the missing ingredient of agape love pivot the disturbing trajectories of child abuse and neglect in our communities.

Young parents need to be better supported, toddlers need access to quality playgroups and play spaces, and families need safer cyberspaces. Families are the building blocks on which communities either thrive or disintegrate. They need to be protected and do not need to be undermined by legislative attempts that limit their ability to nurture their children in the way they know to be best in their situation.

Some are unintentionally squeezing the life out of families by cyber-muzzling those who are seeking to live by the Word of God and putting pressure on governments to implement misguided agendas. That doesn't mean we need to succumb to their bullying and give up beliefs that have been tried and tested over many centuries. St Paul was once such an ideological zealot. He didn't use social media, stoning and jailing was his preferred option for getting rid of troublesome

Christians. He actively instigated terrorizing campaigns in order to curb their influence.

What happened to Paul on the way to Damascus can still happen among the ideological zealots of today. We can find examples of some who have pivoted their once strongly held position on popular platforms such as YouTube. The Jesus revolution Paul and others went on to champion still continues today.

After the resurrection, those who witnessed it understandably couldn't stop talking about it. Many of the early apostles were thrown into prison by the authorities because they were disrupting the prevailing narrative of the time. It didn't stop them. An angel opened the gates of the prison and led them out (Acts 5:17-20). The religious leaders soon caught up with them again and brought them to trial.

They were furious that they kept talking about the crucifixion and the resurrection and wanted to silence them by executing them. Their lives were saved when Gamaliel, an influential member of their governing body, pointed out that if Jesus was really dead then the movement would eventually die out with him. If he wasn't, then they were actually fighting against God and that would prove to be futile. The Sanhedrin had to agree with him so they ordered the disciples not to speak about Jesus and let them go. They immediately continued to proclaim the message of the cross and resurrection.

The movement didn't die because its founder remains alive and the work of proclaiming the message he brought goes on until he returns. Lasing security can only be fully found when we put our trust in the One who made us and who has good plans and purposes for our lives. Because Jesus is still alive today we have nothing to fear if our security is founded in his redemption.

Can it still happen today?

Were the events recorded in the book of Acts simply some miraculous things God did two thousand years ago to get the *Ekklesia* started and have ceased to happen since? The reality is that acts of disciples have been recorded since that time and are still being recorded to the present day. In one of many examples, the persecution of Christians in China has been very intense since Mao's 1949 revolution but many miraculous events have occurred over recent decades and the Chinese church has not only survived but expanded by tens of millions.

One fascinating testimony that has been documented is the account of Brother Yun we can read in the book *The Heavenly Man*. He was imprisoned and beaten a number of times for his evangelistic work as he responded to a call to announce the gospel across China. He managed to continue to do this for twenty years at a time when such activity was strictly forbidden by the regime.

At one time in prison, his legs had been so badly fractured that he could barely walk when he heard God speak to him "This is the hour of your salvation". So sure was he of God's voice that he immediately shuffled to his feet and told a guard he needed to go to the toilet. The guard ordered a designated prisoner to carry him to the toilet which he did. In a series of miraculous events, or of magnificent timing, depending on which way you want to look at it, he then walked through two highly secure iron gates and out onto the road, caught a taxi, and escaped, eventually making it across the border (Hattaway, 2020).

Brother Yun has continued to serve God outside of China since that time and shared accounts of his many experiences of torture and triumph which you can find on platforms such as YouTube. Many accounts of miraculous events have surfaced from persecuted churches over recent decades and indeed over centuries.

The Chinese **underground house church movement** is a remarkable example of pockets of community transformation under fierce resistance from a totalitarian government. Some estimates are that there are now over 100 million Christians in China and that is far many more than there were before the cultural revolution.

It took three centuries until the time of the Emperor Constantine in 306-337AD for the embryonic communities of the early church to develop to the point of transforming whole nations. The faith was at first embraced by a few prominent leaders who formed expressions of *Ekklesia* that were to eventually transform whole communities and nations. The challenge for the *Ekklesia* of today is to develop small gatherings or micro churches (Mathew 18:19-20) made up of people working together in each of the spheres of influence including government, education, family services, media, sport, entertainment, and business.

That has been the agenda of the current cultural neo-Marxist movements that have been very successful in influencing national agendas in recent decades. Jesus' call to make disciples of all nations needs to go far beyond Sunday worship. Churches need to become apostolic centres that help deploy the Body of Christ to be a network of activists, spreading the message of the cross and participating in reforming fragmented cities and nations overwhelmed by intergenerational trauma. We see something of this being played out in the Old Testament *Book of Daniel,* in the journeys of St Paul with Barnabus, Silas, and Timothy, and in the Jesus Revolution of the sixties and seventies.

What can not be ignored in all this is the **agency of the Spirit** at work. When the apostles were questioned about the resurrection they answered that they and the Holy Spirit were witnesses to these events (Acts 5:32). They told their inquisitors that the Spirit is God's gift to those who obey him, and the same applies today. In order to effect significant change the agency of the Spirit is needed to equip believers to radically love across all spheres of influence if we are to see significant change.

In the past many churches have been reluctant to support young people in their communities who have sought after being filled with the Spirit. Some have aggressively discouraged this from happening with spurious theological arguments and attempts to dissuade those hungry for more of God. Somewhat like the religious leaders at the time of Pentecost, they have strategised to curb the activity of the Spirit for fear of losing control of their members.

The long hair and smelly clothes of the sixties and seventies have been replaced by the coloured hair and gender-diverse clothing of the twenties. Will the churches open their hearts to those who are searching for meaning by exploring non-binary identity? Will we steward the movement of the Holy Spirit that releases power to change hardened hearts and transform broken lives? Will churches be the havens of agape love that are needed to bring healing and break the cycle of intergenerational trauma?

There is a revealing account in Acts 8 of what happened in once marginalised Samaria after Pentecost when the disciples were scattered as the church in Jerusalem was intensely persecuted. Many responded to Philip's proclamation of the good news and the accompanying healings that followed and were baptized. When the apostles in Jerusalem heard about this they sent Peter and John who prayed for them to receive the Holy Spirit who had not yet come on any of them.

When they placed their hands on them they received the Spirit. A well-known magician saw what happened and he offered money to Peter and John in exchange for the ability to do the same. Peter responded abruptly by saying that you can never buy the gift of God with money and that his heart was not right before God. He told the magician that needed to repent because he was full of bitterness and captive to sin.

Often we need the ministry of more mature disciples in order to help us in the process of being filled with the Spirit. Our hearts need to be right before God and we need to be free from bitterness and captivity to sin. The Alpha Course[1] is a resource that originated in 1977 and has been developed extensively to walk us through this process. By 2018 it was operating in over 100 countries and in over 100 languages, with more than 24 million people having taken the course. It is free and can be accessed in person, online, or hybrid. and continues to spread worldwide.

Supporting families

---

1.   https://alpha.org/

How can communities better support current generations of parents and children in other practical ways? The message about the importance of the early years is beginning to filter into the general community but more remains to be done. Decisions parents make about the kind of environment they provide for their developing children reflect their understanding of the significance of the early years. We'd have to say that much more needs to be done in terms of raising awareness of the developmental trajectory of children in the first one thousand days of life.

Support for vulnerable families is needed across all organisations they engage with including playgroups, preschools, faith communities, schools, and services. For those most vulnerable as well as professional services, **family hubs** can be a great asset (Brettig, 2020). They usually offer a range of playgroups, parenting groups, perinatal support groups, and 'soft entry' activities that are attractive and readily engage parents. They also link parents with professional services by providing easy access through on-site services or support with making appointments.

Significant government funding is usually needed if a comprehensive range of services are to be offered and management provided by Non-Government Organisations with local knowledge usually works best. Local faith communities can provide scaled-down versions of family hubs with a focus on providing supported playgroups and parenting groups as well as the provision of information about other services available in the local community. They can also offer opportunities for spiritual development through music and movement activities for children, parenting support, and spiritual growth opportunities for parents.

If it takes a village to raise a child then we need adults to work together as a team to raise physically, socially, emotionally, and spiritually healthy children. This is particularly true for parents, but it is also true for children, carers, grandparents, extended family, teachers, service providers, etc. Resources and mentoring are needed to support the development of team parenting skills, especially at a time when individualism is dominating much of the landscape.

Accommodation for families in crisis is an area of service NGOs need to engage with in partnership with the government to support homeless families including those impacted by domestic violence. Some church communities attempt this without government support but the issues of those homeless are usually too complex without the provision of longer-term ongoing supported accommodation. Dispossessed families need to be stabilised and re-established in communities where they can receive ongoing support as well as make contributions to others when they become reconnected in a new and more supportive environment.

On another level, **nutrition** is very important for healthy child development, and providing healthy food for budget-stressed households or breakfast clubs at schools are other practical ways to support vulnerable families. The whole system of parental control, advertising on television, social media accessibility to children, what's on offer at school canteens, and what is taught and modelled in schools needs to be addressed in the challenge of getting children to eat healthy foods.

Social and emotional development is also a key area where community-based initiatives can play a key role in schools. They can support teachers and provide resources to improve the social and emotional skills of children, as well as help connect parents with resources in their local communities. Many teachers are overburdened with the demands of having to take on default parenting roles and more support is needed from community groups in partnership with the government if outcomes for children are to be improved.

We are living in a time of immense social, emotional, and spiritual upheaval as families struggle to cope with an avalanche of pressures brought about by community disintegration and the pitfalls of emerging technologies. Ultimately we need to be engaged in systemic change by building healing communities[2] (Nova, 2021) if we are to lessen the frequent re-traumatisation occurring in the lives of those who have been significantly impacted by early years trauma.

Using social media

How can those involved in supporting families use popular online media to engage parents and support them in their vital role? Facebook has the advantage of offering instant support in a way that traditional community service models cannot. Weekly or fortnightly face-to-face visits can be challenging in terms of time, finances, and logistics which can exclude working mums. So although face-to-face programs are preferable and it is important for young mums to attend these, sometimes this may not be possible due to sickness, pandemics,

---

2.   https://www.researchgate.net/publication/
352368391_An_Action_Plan_to_build_healing_communities

or other issues, and having a Facebook community allows mums continuous access to support in times of need.

As well as crisis management, Facebook also gives young mums the opportunity to discuss child development, and parenting skills and seek general support and friendship. Mentors can monitor discussions, giving them the opportunity to guide young mums, provide positive feedback and help build a strong online community. Mentors can also post research-based information about optimal child development such as how to build quality relationships and the importance of such relationships on children's development.

Information can be made more easily accessible to provide insight into better parenting, and links to more in-depth information can be posted for mums who want to know more. If carefully crafted, to be short yet informative, such information will be more readily available to young mums, and add to their understanding and knowledge base about child development and parenting.

A limitation of using platforms such as Facebook groups as a form of communication and support for families is that it can make them vulnerable to members bullying one another and posting abusive or inappropriate comments. When using these platforms, clear guidelines about acceptable behaviour and netiquette must be prioritized, explained to all members, and managed. Administrators need to monitor and moderate breaches and ensure they have clear guidelines, policies, and protocols in place.

Instagram, Tic Tok, etc can also be used for substantive parenting support. Clearly, these platforms come with surveillance concerns as localities, preferences, and identities are stored by the providers. X offers an abbreviated platform that is potentially useful when used to share links to more substantial support such as can be found in websites or online videos. The implication in all this for family support is that we need to make relevant information available through family-friendly websites and other media available online. The Australian Government's Raising Children Network[3] website is an example of a comprehensive, collaborative effort to make reliable parenting information accessible to families.

Some guidelines for family screen time

There are a lot of great websites that can contribute to supporting parents in their roles. Here are some common suggestions to help families regulate the screen time of their children.

· Sit with kids regularly during screen time, monitor what they're watching, and talk to them about what's being presented.

· Make children earn their screen time. Ensure they've done their homework, played outside for a set time, and cleaned up their areas before allowing them, say, 30 minutes on the computer.

· For younger kids, stick to shows with pro-social messages and coherent storylines.

· Create screen-free times. Choose a place where all devices have to go at dinnertime, for example, and insist that no one in the family be allowed to check messages.

· Model healthy screen use. Set your own limits.

· Put off personal screen use until after the children are in bed.

---

3.   https://raisingchildren.net.au/

· Make children's bedrooms screen-free zones, free of TVs and computers, as well as free from mobile phones after bedtime.

· Talk about commercials and advertising and what's real and what's marketing fantasy.

· Listen to the news together and talk about the social media "cautionary tales" that tend to crop up.

· Get on the social media sites your kids are on. Even if they won't "friend" you, at least follow some of the same people your kids are following and familiarize yourself with what's on these sites.

Clearly, young children need to be protected from bullying or being groomed on social media and should not be able to access it until they are mature enough to be able to navigate the dangers. There are many apps available that can be helpful for their cognitive development, but screen time should not be used to occupy them with meaningless repetitive activities. Some guidelines for deciding what apps are more useful than others for child development can be found in the ebook Quality Play and Media (Brettig, 2015).[4]

These suggestions will be challenging to put into practice in families who have to work with the highly developed abilities of children to evade parental control. However, they do offer a worthwhile starting point to put in place with children. Parenting is a lifelong process and a reciprocal one, often bringing both joy and heartache to parents and children as they navigate the challenges of raising children on a daily basis.

---

4.   https://childrenandmedia.org.au/resources/ebook-quality-play-and-media-in-childhood-education-and-care

Parents do best for their children when they themselves are living in a good space at peace with God and others. Of course, the road is always going to be bumpy and the challenges of living in a digital world constantly being contrived to attract our attention and impact our behavioural choices is not easy for parents or for children.

We all need to work hard at not being controlled by digital platforms and the AI technology behind them. To do this, and gain from the benefits without falling for the pitfalls we need much wisdom to navigate our way. We also need laws to keep AI away from the malicious intent of bad actors. It's rapidly becoming easier to rely on the algorithms of AI more than God. Much discernment is needed to know how to draw the line and be guided by actual God rather than surrender control to the dodgy digital gods so rapidly taking over so much of our lives.

Living by the Logos

The contribution of Christianity to our present way of life has been enormous. Whether we are living it, or whether we are living from its foundations and spending our lives in pursuit of meaningless activities, we can not deny its influence on civilisation as we know it. Putting it into practice is challenging and not the way well travelled by most of us. That is why in these pages we have included a look at what it means to examine the heart and live by the Spirit. These are essential elements that have often been obscured in much of a churchianity that has been ritualised and deconstructed over many centuries.

The *Ekklesia* that Jesus is building relies on his followers obeying his teaching, not because he demands it but because of the loving relationship he has with us (John 3:16, 14:23-24). The Greek word used here for teaching is *logos.* It was originally used by Greek philosophers to mean the rational principle that gave order to the cosmos. It came to mean the agency by which God created the world and by which revelation comes to God's people.

The *Logos* is teaching that has always been true (John 8:31-32) and in fact, has always been (John 1:1). The Master said we will know the truth if we follow his teaching and the truth will set us free because he indeed is the truth (John 14:6) who has always been. He is much more than a good teacher, he is the *Logos* who came in the form of a human being (John 1:14).

Many other religions include a lot of the teaching revealed in the *Logos.* CS Lewis developed a concept from Chinese thought, the *Tao,* which conceptualised the way in which the universe operates. "It is the doctrine of objective value, the belief that certain attitudes are really true, and others really false, to the kind of thing the universe is and the kind of things we are". Most religions have some commonality in this sense.

What is different about Christianity however, is that forgiveness of sin and salvation has been accomplished on the cross of Christ and is a gift to those who receive it by grace through faith, rather than by us trying to better ourselves through our own efforts (Ephesians 2:8-10). Most religions, and indeed most self-help offerings, entreat us to better ourselves and make up for our failings by trying harder rather than by receiving the forgiveness freely available to us because of what Jesus has done.

That seems an unbelievably free gift to sophisticated minds that are always trying to justify themselves. The reality that Christ has done what is required does not sit easily for us in a world where we are used to incessant retribution and shaming for wrongdoing. Receiving the gift of salvation by grace through faith profoundly changes us as we begin to become more like the creatures we were created to be. Our lives become more realigned with the *Logos* when the Holy Spirit works a change in our hearts and minds as we learn to live a life of worship, that includes acts of service and substantial meditation on the Word of God.

The internal consistency of the books of the Bible is remarkable and the likelihood of the prophecies in it being fulfilled as they have been has been calculated by astrophysicist Hugh Ross[5] (Ross, 2003) to be $1:10^{138}$. Prophecies about the central events in the life of Jesus can be found in the Old Testament from his virgin birth at Bethlehem, through his flight to Egypt, life in Nazareth, healing of the sick, betrayal by a friend, condemnation as a criminal, and details about the crucifixion and his resurrection on the third day.

Some 4,500 manuscripts of the New Testament in the original Greek dating back to the second century CE (or AD as it was once known) can be examined today. Carbon dating revealed that manuscripts from the Old Testament including the entire book of Isaiah, discovered by a Bedouin shepherd in a secluded cave on the north shore of the Dead Sea in 1947, dated back to the second century BC. The evidence for the

---

5.   https://reasons.org/explore/publications/articulos/fulfilled-prophecy-evidence-for-the-reliability-of-the-bible

authenticity of the books of the Bible is very extensive, as those who seriously research its accuracy soon discover.

Putting the Word of God into practice sometimes runs counter to what is trending and leads to conflict with popular narratives but that does not mean we need to try to somehow change the truth of it. To do so is arrogance and folly. Trends change over time but the *Logos* does not change. Why do so many rage against those who stand up for what is taught in the *Logos?*

The stoning of the first martyr Stephen sheds some light on this. His accusers listened intently to his extensive exposition of the Old Testament writings but when he pointed out that they had betrayed and killed Jesus the sinless one and not obeyed their law, they were furious, covered their ears, yelled at the top of their voices, rushed at him, dragged him out of the city and stoned him to death (Acts 7).

Guilt does not sit comfortably with any of us because we are all in need of the forgiveness made possible through the Redeemer. God is the number one enemy of those with ambitions to dominate others with their agendas. It is the case for those disregarding human rights in developing their totalitarian states as it is for those who oppose any alternative views to their prescribed agendas.

If we don't seriously seek to discover what is on God's agenda and attempt to formulate our own we end up trying to fight against God. There is no greater force or influence on earth at work among us than the power of God, but it comes to us at a cost. Standing for the truth in agape love sometimes means being misunderstood and willing to suffer abuse.

If Jesus has truly risen from the grave and is alive today then we all need to make a response to his presence. Either we block our ears and make threats against anyone who dares mention his name or we eventually surrender to his grace and forgiveness.

When the Lord called St Paul he said he would show him how much he would suffer for carrying his name across the known world (Acts 9:15-16). When Paul was converted his own people tried to kill him in Damascus where it happened and later in Jerusalem. He was imprisoned, *flogged, stoned, became shipwrecked, and endured many other hardships (2 Corinthians 11:16-23).* That did not stop him from completing the task he had been given, spending his time in prison writing the letters we can read today, and continuing to boldly proclaim the Logos when he was let out of prison.

In the Greek New Testament, there are two words *logos* and *rhema* that both mean 'word'. The *Logos* is the unchanging self-existent Word of God, God's counsel through eternity. The *rhema* is a Word orchestrated by the Holy Spirit that is spoken into specific situations and comes to us personally. Through a *rhema,* God guides us in the walk of faith into which he has called us. A *rhema* that is appropriate for one believer may not be for another or indeed the same believer at another time in life. It is given to individuals by the Spirit who knows their capacity and needs at particular times and in particular situations (Prince, 1977).

We can readily see the application of the *rhema* and the *logos* at work in the life of Paul. He instructed those who accompanied him to proclaim the *Logos* at all times (2 Timothy 4:2). In Acts 22:1-21 he describes how he was guided in his work of proclaiming the *Logos*. In this account, he mentions five occasions on which the Lord spoke to him giving him *rhema* instructions with specific directions regarding what he was called to be doing. It is significant that Paul was not one of the disciples who spent three years accompanying the Master and this account reveals one of the profound ways the risen Good Shepherd continues to guide those who are called to follow in his footsteps (John 10:27).

Interestingly, Paul's testimony was followed by a similar, though much more animated conversation to the one we had in chapter three about worldviews (Acts 23:6-11). One Jewish sect believed in miracles angels and spirits and another did not, and a violent dispute erupted among members of the ruling Sanhedrin. Paul was reassured in the precarious days that lay ahead by another *rhema* word he received from God on the night following all the commotion.

The perplexing question of modernity is the old question of Pilate, how do we know what is true? What is true is what always has been true, and has been shown to be true, over the entirety of history. It is not necessarily what is trending on the internet and echoing through the chambers of cyberspace, or gets us invited to conferences or elite social gatherings when we acquiesce to misguided political correctness.

The more we tell the truth the more we align ourselves with the *Logos*, the more we become **free from being manipulated**. That comes at the cost of risking being marginalised and cancelled from some popular conversations. The more we lie, however, the more we become imprisoned in and diminished in a world of seductive untruths and eroding foundations.

That is why the *Ekklesia* needs to remain free to teach the full counsel of the Logos uncensored by political interference. At the same time, its spokespersons need to contribute considered opinions in the light of a thorough examination of the *Logos,* rather than engage in crass retorts. That is the arena in which we need to retain the separation of church and state in a functional democracy.

The authenticity of the Word of God has been validated over many centuries and, in addressing trending narratives, it needs to be taken seriously or the consequences may well be dire. History has demonstrated this time and time again as prophets have warned of disastrous consequences when nations attempt to live unaligned with the *Logos*. In the beginning was the Word and in the end, the Book of Revelation depicts the ultimate triumph of the *Logos* over those conspiring to destroy its influence (Revelation 19: 11-21). We do well to give it serious attention.

There are many complex factors that contribute to the malaise of intergenerational trauma many families in many nations are experiencing today. Trauma that is passed down for generations lies at the heart of disintegrating communities. Child-friendly policies, complex trauma therapies, and family support services being developed contribute significantly to making a difference, but we are not likely to see a change of concerning trajectories of abuse and neglect unless we recognise that we also need to address a spiritual malaise.

Not many have issues about including spirituality in the conversation if we are talking about Aboriginal, Buddhist, Hindu, or any other number of spiritualities, but readily discount what has to be the most practised, researched, and validated spirituality of all time. Dealing with uncomfortable truths is always challenging. We see this is as the international community grapples with the implications of climate change, and we also need to come to terms with it in relation to the factors impacting family and community disintegration.

The bottom line is that we all need a regular heart check-up if we are to put aside entrenched dysfunction and self-interest and pursue lasting change. To follow alternative paths that may be trending but untrue is not a good option. Dealing with what separates us from God frees us to hear the voice of the Good Shepherd and live according to His revealed instructions. When we do that we can contribute to building healing communities and bring hope to a rapidly changing world.

Further Reading

Anderson, Neil T. (1990). The Bondage Breaker. Monarch Publications. https://www.logos.com/product/210704/the-bondage-breaker

Ano, Gene G. & Vasconcelles, Erin B. (2005). Religious coping and psychological adjustment to stress. A meta-analysis. PubMed.

Arndt, William F. & Gingrich, F Wilbur. (1979). *A Greek-English Lexicon of the New Testament and Other Early Christian Literature*. Second Edition. University of Chicago Press.

Beauregard, Mario. & O'Leary, Denise. (2008). *The Spiritual Brain - A Neuroscientist's Case for the Existence of the Soul*. Harper One. https://www.harpercollins.com/products/the-spiritual-brain-mario-beauregarddenyse-oleary?variant=32206447575074

Blainey, Geoffrey (2011). *A Short History of Christianity*. Penguin. https://www.penguin.com.au/books/a-short-history-of-christianity-9781742534169

Brettig, Karl (ed). (2020). *Building Stronger Communities with Children and Families (2nd Edition)*. Scholars Publishing. https://www.cambridgescholars.com/product/978-1-5275-4145-0

Brettig, Karl (ed). (2015). *Quality Play and Media*. ACCM. https://childrenandmedia.org.au/resources/ebook-quality-play-and-media-in-childhood-education-and-care

Davediuk Gingrich, Heather. (2020). Restoring the Shattered Self. IVP Academic; Second edition. https://www.ivpress.com/restoring-the-shattered-self

Dowley, Tim (Ed). (1977). *The History of Christianity*. Lion Publishing.

Foster, Richard. (1978). *Celebration of Discipline*. Harper Collins. https://renovare.org/books/celebration-of-discipline

Fagan, Patrick. (2006). https://www.heritage.org/civil-society/report/why-religion-matters-even-more-the-impact-religious-practice-social-stability

Future of Life Institute. (2023). *An Open Letter*. https://futureoflife.org/open-letter/pause-giant-ai-experiments/

Garroutte, Eva Marie et al. (2003). *Spirituality and attempted suicide among American Indians*. https://pubmed.ncbi.nlm.nih.gov/12614706/

Guy-Evans, Olivia. (2021). Amygdala *Function and Location*. *https:*//www.simplypsychology.org/amy<gdala.html[6]

Harari, Yuval. (2015). *Homo Deus A Brief History of Tomorrow*. Vintage. https://www.ynharari.com/book/homo-deus/

Hart, Max. (1988*). A Story of Fire Continued - Aboriginal Christianity*. New Creation Publications.

Hattaway, Paul. (2020). The Heavenly> *Man - A remarkable true story of Chinese Christian Brother Yun*. Kregel Publications.

Hinton, Geoffrey. (2023). https://www.cbsnews.com/news/godfather-of-artificial-intelligence-weighs-in-on-the-past-and-potential-of-artificial-intelligence/?ftag=CNM-00-10aab8d&linkId=207086575

Hinton et al (2023). Statement on AI Risk. https://www.safe.ai/statement-on-ai-risk

Holland, Tom. (2019). *Dominion the Making of the Western Mind*. Little Brown. https://www.littlebrown.co.uk/titles/tom-holland/dominion-50th-anniversary-edition/9780349145273/

Kahane, Adam. (2018). *Power and Love - A Theory and Practice of Social Change*. Penguin. https://www.penguin.com.au/books/power-and-love-9781605093048

Keller, Timothy. (2022). *Forgive*. Penguin.

Keller, Timothy. (2022). *The Decline and Renewal of the American Church*. Gospel in Life.

Langberg, Dianne. (2015). *Suffering and the Heart of God*. New Growth Press.

https://newgrowthpress.com/christian-books/biblical-counseling-books/suffering-and-the-heart-of-god-how-trauma-destroys-and-christ-restores/

Laurie, Greg. & Vaughn, Ellen. (2017). *Jesus Revolution - How God Transformed an Unlikely Generation and How He can do it again Today*. Baker Books. http://bakerpublishinggroup.com/books/jesus-revolution/387952

Lawrence, Brother. (1895), *The Practice of the Presence of God*. Revell.

Lennox, John. (2020). 2084 - *Artificial Intelligence and the Future of Humanity*. Zondervan. https://www.youtube.com/watch?v=bvf_n6Cnp8s

---

6.   https://www.simplypsychology.org/amy%3Cgdala.html

Lewis. CS. (2009). *Mere Christianity. Revised and Enlarged Edition*, Harper Collins, https://www.harpercollins.com/products/mere-christianity-c-s-lewis?variant=32123686158370

Ludwig, David J. & Jacob. Mary R., (2014). *Christian Concepts for Care*. Concordia Publishing House. https://www.cph.org/christian-concepts-for-care-ebook-edition

Massengill, Rebekah P., & MacGregor, Carol Ann. (2012). *Religious Nonaffiliation and Schooling The Educational Trajectories of Three Types of Religious Nones*. Emerald Group Publishing.

Meyer, Stephen C. (2019). *The Return of the God Hypothesis*. Harper Collins.

Miller, Lisa. (2021). *The Awakened Brain*. Allen Lane. https://www.penguin.co.uk/books/313885/the-awakened-brain-by-miller-lisa/9780141991030

Netchev, Simeon. (2022). "The Growth of Christianity in the Roman Empire." World History Encyclopedia. https://www.worldhistory.org/image/15640/the-growth-of-christianity-in-the-roman-empire/

Nova Smart Solutions. (2021). *An Action Plan to Build Healing Communities*.

Olsen, Steen (2020). *Jacob's Ladder - Missional church in the 1970s*. https://www.openbookhowden.com.au/product/jacobs-ladder/

Oman, D., & Thoresen, C. E. (2005). *Do Religion and Spirituality Influence Health?* In R. F. Paloutzian & C. L. Park (Eds.), Handbook of the psychology of religion and spirituality (pp. 435–459). The Guilford Press. https://psycnet.apa.org/record/2006-00771-024

Peck, M Scott. (1997). *The Road Less Travelled and Beyond*. Simon & Schuster.

Prince, Derek (1977). *Faith to Live By*. https://www.derekprince.com/books/faith-to-live-by

Rew, Lynn, & Yong, Joel W. (2006). *A Systematic Review of Associations Among Religiosity Spirituality and Adolescent Heath Attitudes and Behaviors*. PubMed.

Ross, Hugh. (2003). *Fulfilled Prophecy: Evidence for the Reliability of the Bible*. https://reasons.org/explore/publications/articles/fulfilled-prophecy-evidence-for-the-reliability-of-the-bible

Schlink, Basilea. (1959). *Repentance the Joy filled Life*. Evangelical Sisterhood of Mary.

Shortz, J. L., & Worthington, E. L. (1994). *Young adults' recall of religiosity, attributions, and coping in parental divorce*. Journal for the Scientific Study of Religion, 33(2), 172–179. https://doi.org/10.2307/1386603

Silvoso. Ed. (2017). *Ekklesia - Rediscovering God's Instrument for Global Transformation*. Chosen. http://bakerpublishinggroup.com/books/ekklesia/384625

Sinha, Jill. Witmer., Cnaan, Ram., & Gelles, Richard,. (2007). *Adolescent Risk Behaviours and Religion Findings from a National Study*.

Sparks, Jack. (1974). *God's Forever Family - Christians in the midst of a revolutionary society*. Zondervan.

Stark, Rodney & Wang, Xiuhua (2015). *A Star in the East*. Templeton Press.

Tze Ming Ng, Peter, Tai Leung, Wing. & King Tong Mack, Vaughan, (2021). *Christian Mind in the Emerging World - Faith Integration in Asian Contexts and Global Perspectives*. Cambridge Scholars Publishing. https://www.cambridgescholars.com/product/978-1-5275-1649-6

Walker, Donald F., Courtois, Christine A., Aten, Jamie D. & Hathaway, William. (2014). *Spiritually Oriented Psychotherapy for Trauma 1st Edition*. American Psychological Association.

Willard, Dallas. (2021). *Renovation of the Heart*. Navpress.

Wright, L. S., Frost, C. J., & Wisecarver, S. J. (1993). *Church attendance, meaningfulness of religion, and depressive symptomatology among adolescents*. Journal of Youth and Adolescence, 22(5), 559–568. https://doi.org/10.1007/BF01537716

Yaden, David B. & Newberg, Andrew. (2023). *The Varieties of Spiritual Experience: 21st Century Research and Perspectives*. Oxford University Press.

Scripture quotations from the *New International Version* © 1973 *International Bible Society* with reference to *Young's Analytical Concordance to the Bible* © 1970 *William B Eerdmans Publishing Company*.

About the Author

Karl Brettig has edited/authored a number of publications including 'Building Stronger Communities with Children and Families' and 'Quality Play and Media'. He has worked in secondary and tertiary state education services and held leadership positions in family and community services and faith communities in South Australia. At Adelaide University he majored in Psychology and English and has postgraduate qualifications in education and theology.

Read more at https://karlbrettig.wordpress.com/.